Everyday
WORLD WAR I

WITH CROSS-CURRICULAR ACTIVITIES IN EACH CHAPTER

WALTER A. HAZEN

A GOOD YEAR BOOK™

GOOD YEAR BOOKS
Tucson, Arizona

Photo Credits

Front cover: Royal Aircraft Factory SE5, single seater with Vickers and Lewis gun, powered by Hispano-Suiza, 1914-18 by Withams, B. (20th century) ©Private Collection/ The Bridgeman Art Library. Sentry in a Little Advanced Post in the Champagne region, 1916 (b/w photo) by Moreau, Jacques (b.1887) ©Archives Larousse, Paris, France/ Giraudon/ The Bridgeman Art Library. **Interior:** 2: P.J. Gallais et Cie, Paris, Library of Congress. 3: U.S. Food Administration poster, U.S. National Archives and Records Administration. (NARA) 4: Signal Corps photo, NARA. 10: George Grantham Bain collection, Library of Congress. 11: Courtesy of Photos of the Great War: World War I Image Archive. 13: War Department photo, NARA. 18: Library of Congress. 19: George Grantham Bain collection, Library of Congress. 20: George Grantham Bain collection, Library of Congress. 26: War Department photo, NARA. 27: War Department photo, NARA. 28: Courtesy of the National Museum of the United States Air Force. 29: NARA. 34: NARA. 35: U.S. Food Administration poster, NARA. 37: NARA. 42: War Department photo, NARA. 44: NARA. 45: Signal Corps photo, NARA. 50: Library of Congress. 51: NARA. 52: War Department photo, NARA. 53: War Department photo, NARA. 58: U.S. Food Administration poster, NARA. 59: NARA. 61: George Grantham Bain collection, Library of Congress. 66: U.S. Food Administration photo, NARA. 67: NARA. 69: U.S. Food Administration poster, NARA. 75: Courtesy of Photos of the Great War: World War I Image Archive. 76: U.S. Food Administration photo, NARA. 77: all War Department photos, NARA. 82: NARA. 84: Signal Corps photo, NARA.

Dedication

To the memory of my brother, Walton.

Acknowledgments

Grateful acknowledgment is extended to Roberta Dempsey, Editorial Director at Good Year Books, who patiently guided me through this addition to the "Everyday Life" series. Without her advice and support, this book would not have been possible.

I would also like to thank Helen Fisher, Publisher at Good Year Books, for giving me the opportunity to continue the "Everyday Life" series. Her support and confidence in me is likewise appreciated.

Good Year Books

Our titles are available for most basic curriculum subjects plus many enrichment areas. For more Good Year Books, contact your local bookseller or educational dealer. For a complete catalog with information about other Good Year Books, please contact:

Good Year Books
P. O. Box 91858
Tucson, Arizona 85752-1858
www.goodyearbooks.com

Editor: Roberta Dempsey
Cover Design: Dan Miedaner
Interior Design: Dan Miedaner

Copyright © 2006 Walter A. Hazen
Printed in the United States of America.
All rights reserved.

ISBN-10: 1-59647-074-7
ISBN-13: 978-1-59647-074-3

1 2 3 4 5 6 7 8 9 - ML - 09 08 07 06

Library of Congress Cataloging-in-Publication Data

Hazen, Walter A.
    Everyday life : World War I : with cross-curricular activities in each chapter / Walter A. Hazen.
        p. cm.
    Includes bibliographical references.
    ISBN-13: 978-1-59647-074-3
    ISBN-10: 1-59647-074-7
    1. World War, 1914-1918--Textbooks. 2. World War, 1914-1918--Study and teaching--Activity programs. I. Title. II. Title: World War I. III. Title: World War One. IV. Title: World War 1.

D522.7.H39 2006
940.3--dc22

2006043436

Table of Contents

Table of Contents *continued*

Introduction

People of the time called it the Great War. Before it was over, it would involve about forty nations from around the globe. When it began, spirited soldiers marched proudly off to battle, confident in their leaders' assurances that the war would last only a matter of weeks or months. No one was prepared for a bloody struggle that would last for four years. When it finally did end, people everywhere began referring to it as "the war to end all wars."

The start of World War I should not have surprised anyone. Although the assassination of a member of the Austrian royal family set it off, decades-long distrust and rivalries among nations were the underlying causes. France and Germany had been at odds for decades, and many different peoples in the Balkans were unhappy under the rule of the Ottoman Turks and the Austro-Hungarians. In addition, the nations of Europe were in an arms race, each determined to have a military force second to none. Finally, a race for colonies in Africa and elsewhere only added to the tension. What *is* surprising is that World War I did not break out earlier.

Everyday Life: World War I focuses on the effects the war had on the peoples of Europe and elsewhere. There are battles here, certainly, but they are confined to one chapter. The remaining chapters deal with the lives of soldiers on the battlefronts and civilians on the home fronts. Students will learn what it was like for soldiers to live and fight in muddy trenches, and they will gain an understanding of the hardships and sacrifices faces by civilians at home.

Everyday Life: World War I is unlike most books dealing with the war, and it is a book students should enjoy.

Walter A. Hazen

CHAPTER I

Background and Causes

Wars are not caused by a single incident that occurs at any particular moment, and that was certainly the case with World War I. The "spark" that set off that war was the assassination of Archduke Francis Ferdinand in Bosnia on June 28, 1914. However, the causes of the war are more profound and go back many years before that fateful day in 1914.

Perhaps the main cause of World War I was nationalism—pride in one's country. The purest form of nationalism—swelling with pride at seeing your country's flag or hearing your national anthem—is not likely to lead to war. But other forms of nationalism can and have led to war. One example is the case of America in the eighteenth century, when colonists desiring independence fought against Great Britain. When nationalism is taken to extremes, people develop the feeling that their nation is better than or superior to others. Such a belief has led to armed conflicts since the beginning of written history.

"War is the national industry of Prussia." French World War I propoganda poster depicting Prussia as an octopus whose tentacles are reaching into Europe. ca. 1910–20.

Feelings of nationalism ran high in parts of Europe in the early 1900s. This was particularly true in the Balkans. The Balkans are a group of countries that form a peninsula in southeast Europe that lies between the Adriatic and Black seas. This area includes the present-day countries of Greece, Bulgaria, Albania, and all of what was once Yugoslavia. A small part of Turkey is also considered part of the area. People of many nationalities live in the region: Greeks, Romanians, Albanians, Turks, and Slavs. Included in the latter group are Serbs, Croats, Macedonians, Bulgarians, and Slovenes.

In the years leading up to World War I, few of the ethnic groups mentioned above enjoyed independence. Most were subjects of the Austro-Hungarian Empire, which included the combined monarchies of Austria and Hungary and parts of what are now Poland, Slovakia, the Czech Republic, and Yugoslavia. Within its borders lived Serbs, Croats, Poles, Czechs, Italians, and Romanians who were unhappy under Austrian rule and wanted to govern themselves.

Nationalism of a different sort characterized the Ottoman Empire. The Ottoman Empire—named for its founder, Osman—was the empire of the Turks. Through the centuries, the Turks had extended their rule over Greece, Albania, and Bulgaria, and they once posed a serious threat to all of Europe. But by the nineteenth century, their empire had begun to fall apart. First, Greece became an independent nation in 1829. Then in 1878, the nations of Serbia, Montenegro, and Romania were carved from the disintegrating empire. Finally, in 1908, Bulgaria became independent, and the Turks were left with only a fraction of their former European holdings. Small wonder that the Ottoman Empire became known as the "sick man of Europe."

Other nations sought to take advantage of the Turks' weakness. Germany wanted to build a railroad from Berlin through the Balkans to Baghdad. Control of the Turkish city of Constantinople would offer Russians the trade port they had long needed. And France, Great Britain, and Austria-Hungary began to cast envious eyes toward the crumbling Turkish Empire. Rivalries among European powers to gain Turkish territory brought the world ever closer to war.

Serbia's ambitions for Turkish land were a case in point. In 1912, Serbia joined Greece, Bulgaria, and Montenegro and attacked the Turks. This was the First Balkan War. Serbia and its allies easily won and divided Macedonia, a region just north of Greece, among themselves. At the same time, Serbia seized Albania. This move greatly alarmed Austria-Hungary. In the eyes of the Austrians, Serbia was becoming too powerful. Backed by Germany and Italy, Austria-Hungary forced the Serbs to declare Albania an independent nation. Thus a much broader war was averted.

U.S. Food Administration educational poster, ca. 1917. Serbia had as much to do with bringing about World War I as any other nation.

Not long after the end of the First Balkan War, the Bulgarians began claiming that they had been cheated out of land. In 1913 the Second Balkan War broke out when Bulgaria attacked Serbia, and Greece, Turkey, and Romania attacked Bulgaria. Bulgaria was soundly defeated, and Serbia ended up doubling its territory. Austria-Hungary viewed these events with great alarm. What would the Serbs try next?

Farther east and north in Europe, nationalism fueled the flames of distrust among the European powers. France had lost the important province of

Alsace-Lorraine to Germany in 1871, and many of the French were determined to get it back. Such tension led both countries to increase the size of their armies. Germany's buildup of its navy prompted Great Britain to view Germany with distrust.

Compared to the other nations of Europe, Russia was a backward country, but the size of its army was a cause for concern. When World War I broke out, the Russians could place more than six million troops in the field. It mattered little that Russia's minister of war, General Sukhomlinov, frowned on modern tactics and openly boasted that he "had not read a military manual in twenty-five years." It also mattered little that the Russian army was ill-trained and poorly equipped. What did matter was that Russia's army was much larger than that of other European nations, which caused considerable worry in Germany and Austria-Hungary.

Italian mounted infantry in Peking, China, ca. 1900, part of a 19,000-man international expedition sent to China to protect trade rights.

Imperialism was another factor that brought on the war. Imperialism is the policy of strong nations seeking control over weaker ones. In the late nineteenth century, European nations vied for either influence or control of colonies in Africa, Asia, and the Middle East. By the end of the century, a handful of European powers had carved up Africa entirely. Africans fought back as best they could, but they were no match for Europeans with modern weapons. Great Britain took control of Nigeria, Kenya, Uganda, and the Gold Coast. France claimed Algeria, Morocco, Tunisia, and the island of Madagascar off Africa's east coast. Germany seized South West Africa and German East Africa. Italy gobbled up Libya, Eritrea, and Italian Somaliland. Not to be outdone, Portugal claimed Guinea, Mozambique, and Angola. Finally, Belgium seized the Congo in the central part of Africa. By the time World War I broke out, rivalries among the European powers for colonies were intense.

In the mid-nineteenth century, these European powers began to look to China for new colonies. Unlike Africa, China had not yet been carved up and taken over by the European powers. Instead, it was divided into spheres of influence. A sphere of influence is an area where a country controlled trade and

business. Each European nation had exclusive rights in its part of China. The French, Russians, British, Germans, and Portuguese all reaped profits from their share of Chinese trade. The Japanese also got into the act after defeating China in a brief war. The Chinese, to be sure, resented foreign control and meddling, but their nation was too weak to do anything about it.

Nationalism and the competition for colonies led to ever-increasing mistrust among the nations of Europe. The result of such mistrust was the formation of alliances in the late 1800s and early 1900s. An alliance is an agreement among nations to act together and to help each other. If one nation in an alliance is attacked, the other members are pledged to come to its aid.

Two such alliances were formed. Germany and Austria-Hungary had formed the Dual Alliance in 1879. The primary goal of this alliance was to isolate France from the rest of Europe. In 1870 and 1871, Germany had battled France for Alsace-Lorraine, a region between the two countries. Germany had won, but more than ten years later, its leaders still feared France would seek revenge for the defeat. Italy, a fairly weak nation, also feared the possibility of a French attack, so in 1882 Italy joined Germany and Austria-Hungary in what became known as the Triple Alliance.

The second alliance to appear was the Triple Entente, formed in 1907. *Entente* is a French word meaning a "friendly agreement." The Triple Entente grew out of an alliance formed in 1894 between France and Russia. At the time, France needed an ally and Russia needed money. France granted Russia a loan in return for its help should the Triple Alliance pose a threat. In 1907, Great Britain, fearful of Germany's growing navy, joined the two, creating the Triple Entente.

Europe was now divided into two armed camps. Should any two rival powers "come to blows," all six nations would be drawn into the conflict. Thus Europe was on the brink of world war almost a decade before it actually broke out. All that was needed was a spark to set it off—and that spark occurred in Bosnia in the Balkans in June 1914.

Name _____ Date _____

Write a Letter

Pretend you are living somewhere in Europe in the months leading up to World War I. There is a lot of tension between nations, and you are worried about how your life might be affected if war does break out. Write a letter to a friend expressing your thoughts and feelings.

Date _____

Dear _____,

_____

_____

_____

_____

_____

_____

_____

_____

_____

_____

_____

_____

_____

_____

_____

_____

_____

_____

_____

_____

Sincerely,

_____

(Your Name)

Name _____ Date _____

Distinguish between Fact and Opinion

Can you tell the difference between a fact and an opinion? Sometimes it is not easy to do. In our daily conversations, we make statements we think are facts but which in reality are opinions. Facts are things that are true and can be proven; opinions are simply strong beliefs.

Here are statements related to what you read in chapter 1. On the blank line to the left of each, write F if you think the statement is a fact. Write O if you think it is an opinion.

1. ____ World War I might have been prevented had Archduke Francis Ferdinand not been assassinated in 1914.

2. ____ Nationalism was one of the main causes of World War I.

3. ____ Germany's fear that France might seek revenge for previously lost territory helped bring on World War I.

4. ____ World War I could have been avoided had Austria-Hungary granted independence to all the nationalities living within its borders.

5. ____ Great Britain viewed Germany's growing naval power with great alarm.

6. ____ European nations considered the Ottoman Empire to be the "sick man of Europe."

7. ____ France would have most likely attacked Italy had that nation not joined the Triple Alliance.

8. ____ Russia became France's ally in 1894 when the French granted the Russians a loan.

9. ____ Africans benefited greatly as European nations carved up the African continent for their own purposes.

10. ____ Serbia's territorial ambitions did more than anything else to bring on World War I.

11. ____ With the formation of the Triple Entente in 1907, Europe was divided into two armed camps.

Name _____ Date _____

Draw a Map of the Balkan Peninsula

The Balkan region has changed considerably since the outbreak of World War I. With this in mind, draw a map of the Balkan Peninsula as it appears today. Write in the name of each country, along with each capital. Color your map to make it more attractive and to better define boundaries.

Consult a recent encyclopedia or atlas for a modern map of the Balkans. You can also find samples on the Internet.

Include the following countries on your map: Croatia, Bosnia-Herzegovina, Serbia & Montenegro (until 2003 it was known as Yugoslavia), Macedonia, Slovenia, Albania, Bulgaria, and Greece.

Name _____ Date _____

Interpret a Bar Graph

The bar graph shows the number of troops in millions mobilized (called to fight) by six countries at the beginning of World War I.

Review *mean*, *mode*, and *range* in your mathematics text and, using the information from the graph, answer the questions at the bottom of the page.

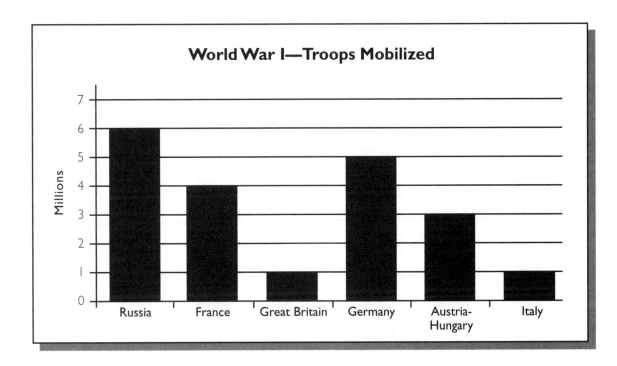

World War I—Troops Mobilized

1. What is the *mean* of the numbers provided? _____

2. Is there a *mode*? _____. If so, write it on this line. _____

3. What is the *range*? _____

4. How many times greater were the forces of Russia than Austria-Hungary?

   _____

5. Which two countries had approximately the same number of troops?

   _____

CHAPTER 2

The Lights Go Out in Europe

Otto von Bismarck, the chancellor (prime minister) of Germany from 1862 to 1888, had predicted that war would break out over "some foolish thing in the Balkans." In 1914, his prediction came to pass with the assassination of Archduke Francis Ferdinand, the heir to the throne of Austria-Hungary.

In June 1914, duty drew the archduke to the Austrian province of Bosnia. The Austro-Hungarian army was participating in maneuvers there, and Ferdinand had no choice but to go to the Bosnian capital of Sarajevo. His position as inspector-general of the Austro-Hungarian army required that he be there.

Archduke Francis Ferdinand with his children, Sophie, Maximillian, and Ernst.

Accompanying Francis Ferdinand to Bosnia was his devoted wife, Countess Sophie. It was a special occasion; the couple were celebrating their fourteenth wedding anniversary. They had no idea, of course, that the day of their visit would be their last day on earth.

Lurking along the route of the archduke's four-car motorcade that fateful morning were seven young Serbians. All were members of a Serbian terrorist group called the Black Hand. The goal of the Black Hand was to create a Greater Serbia by uniting all Serbs in the Balkan area under one rule. But there was a catch; Serbs who lived outside of Serbia were in territories controlled by Austria-Hungary. The Black Hand hoped that if Francis Ferdinand were dead, Austria-Hungary might give up control of these territories.

The seven Serbians who awaited the archduke and his countess that morning were all young. Five were under the age of twenty. The oldest was twenty-seven. Four were students. The others were a teacher, a printer, and a carpenter, respectively. None had previous criminal records. The one thing that bound them together was that they all suffered from tuberculosis. It has been suggested that they agreed to carry out the plot because a sudden death at the hands of the police was preferable to a slow death by a then-incurable disease.

And how could anyone think they could walk right up to an archduke's touring car and shoot him and his wife? Didn't the car have some kind of "bubble" that shielded the occupants? Were there no police or bodyguards?

Until fairly recent times, political figures rode in open cars. Such was the case with President John F. Kennedy when he was assassinated in Dallas in 1963. That day in Sarajevo, there were police around, but the archduke wanted security kept to a minimum. Thousands of soldiers were ordered to stay away from the city that day. Therefore, it was quite easy for the seven conspirators to get to the archduke.

As the archduke's car moved along its route, one young conspirator hurled a bomb at Ferdinand's car. It bounced off. Several policemen and a number of onlookers were injured, but the archduke was unharmed.

The motorcade stopped at city hall for a brief reception. When it got underway again, the motorcade passed five conspirators who simply froze and did nothing. But when the archduke's car reached the point where nineteen-year-old Gavrilo Princip was standing, he stepped forward and fired two shots. One shot hit Ferdinand in the neck. The other hit Sophie in the abdomen. When the archduke realized his wife was dying, he cried: "Sophie dear, Sophie dear! Don't die! Stay alive for our children!" But the countess was dead before they could get her out of the car, and Ferdinand died shortly afterward.

Gavrilo Princip, fired the opening shots of World War I when he killed Archduke Francis Ferdinand and Countess Sophie.

Having carried out the mission, Princip tried to turn the pistol on himself. But someone in the crowd snatched it away before he could fire. He next tried to swallow a cyanide capsule, but it only made him sick. Taken into custody, he was tried, convicted, and sent to prison. He was spared the death penalty because of his youth. Four years later, in April 1918, he died in prison of tuberculosis.

Princip's assassination of Francis Ferdinand ended the uneasy peace in Europe. Within a month, the continent was at war. First, Austria-Hungary declared war on Serbia, blaming that country for hatching the plot to kill the archduke. Shortly afterward, the other countries in the Triple Alliance and Triple Entente followed suit. On August 1, a few days after Russia vowed to come to Serbia's aid, Germany declared war on Russia. Two days later, Germany declared war on France, Russia's ally. On August 4, Great Britain, the third member of the Triple Entente, was drawn into the conflict. All nations now readied their armies for what they thought would be a brief war.

Most wars begin amid much excitement and expectations of quick victory, and World War I was no exception. Every nation expected its warriors to be home safely by the onset of winter. This was especially true in Germany. The confident Germans gave the war no more than four months. Kaiser Wilhelm II told his departing troops that they would be home "before the leaves had fallen from the trees." One German officer went further, telling friends that he fully expected to be eating breakfast at one of Paris's more elegant cafes within a matter of weeks.

Departing German soldiers held similar views, scribbling boastful messages, such as "On to Paris" and "See you again on the Boulevard," on the sides of their transport trains as they departed for battle. They hung out the windows of the cars, waving and shouting as their trains pulled out of stations throughout Germany.

Not to be outdone, German civilians also got into the act. One famous picture of the time shows a young woman marching alongside the troops as they departed for the front. The same picture shows a man who had discarded his straw hat for a German soldier's helmet and marched along with the soldier's rifle on his shoulder.

Similar scenes took place throughout Europe. Huge crowds gathered in European capitals and cheered, sang, and danced. Young men rushed to recruitment offices to enlist. Some actually worried that the fighting would be over before they had a chance to fight. Others saw the war as an opportunity for adventure and a chance to escape from routine jobs. Few seemed to realize the horrors they would soon face.

Nowhere were expectations of success higher than in Russia. Russians were convinced that they would win and argued only about how long it would take. Most said two or three months, and anyone who suggested six months was thought to be an extreme pessimist. One Imperial Guard officer asked the czar's private physician if he should go ahead and pack his full-dress uniform so he would have it for the Russians' triumphal entry into Berlin. How's that for confidence?

In spite of the boasting and party atmosphere, cooler and wiser heads saw what was ahead. For all its swagger and saber-rattling, Germany had the means to produce only enough gunpowder for six months. If a faster method of production had not been discovered, Germany would have been forced to drop out of the war. Even had a sufficient supply of gunpowder been available at the start, Count Helmuth Johannes von Moltke, chief of the German general staff

since 1906, saw what the kaiser and others failed to see: a "long, wearisome struggle," not one that would end in a matter of a few months. The kaiser thought that Great Britain would remain neutral, having no direct interest in what took place on the European continent proper.

France's General Joseph Jacques Joffre shared von Moltke's concern. He foresaw a war of "indefinite duration," pointing out that other nations would surely be drawn into the conflict. The war minister of Great Britain, Lord Horatio Kitchener, agreed. Kitchener predicted the war would last at least three years. He believed it would take that long to beat a nation as strong as Germany to the point of surrender.

No leading official summed it up better than Sir Edward Grey, the British foreign minister. Gazing from the windows of his office as he watched the street lamps being lit on the evening of August 4, he said: "The lamps are going out all over Europe; we shall not see them lit again in our lifetime."

Thus the fighting began in what would become the worst war the world had known until that time. Soon the opposing sides became

An old French couple visit the rubble that was once their home. The German advance left many people homeless.

known as the Central Powers and the Allies. In the beginning, the Central Powers were made up of Germany, Austria-Hungary, and the Ottoman (Turkish) Empire. Italy dropped out of the Triple Alliance before the fighting started, hoping to gain territory at the expense of Austria-Hungary. The Italians would later join the Allies.

The opposition—Great Britain, France, and Russia—became known as the Allies. As the war progressed, the Allies came to include Great Britain, France, Russia (who dropped out of the fighting before the end of the war as the people overthrew their czar), Italy, Belgium, Serbia, the United States, and some twenty other countries around the world. In fact, before the war ended more than four years later, all of Europe and countries on most of the world's other continents would be involved in the conflict that started in Sarajevo that day in 1914.

Name _____ Date _____

Create a Dialogue

Remember that a dialogue is a conversation between two or more persons. With this in mind, create a dialogue that might have taken place at the beginning of World War I between three young men who are weighing the pros and cons of enlisting in their country's army. The three men can be from any of the countries involved at the start of the war. Try to imagine what they might be thinking at this time and what they would say to each other.

_____

_____

_____

_____

_____

_____

_____

_____

_____

_____

_____

_____

_____

_____

_____

_____

_____

_____

_____

_____

_____

_____

_____

_____

_____

_____

_____

_____

_____

Name _____ Date _____

Make False Statements True

All the statements on this page are false. Change the words in *italics* to make them true. Write the replacement words on the lines following the statements.

1. *Joseph Jacques Joffre* was the German chancellor who predicted that World War I would break out in the Balkans. _____

2. Archduke Francis Ferdinand was heir to the throne of *Germany.* _____.

3. *Russia* was accused of hatching the plot to assassinate Francis Ferdinand. _____

4. Francis Ferdinand was assassinated in the province of *Croatia.* _____

5. The statement "The lamps are going out all over Europe; we shall not see them lit again in our lifetime" is attributed to *Count Helmut Johannes von Moltke.*
_____

6. The *Triple Alliance* was made up of France, Russia, and Great Britain. _____

7. Kaiser Wilhelm II was the ruler of *Austria-Hungary.*
_____

8. The European ruler who promised his troops that "they would be home before the leaves had fallen from the trees" was *Czar Nicholas II of Russia.*
_____

9. Most Europeans thought that if war broke out it would last for only a few *years.* _____

10. Gavrilo Princip, who fired the shot that killed Francis Ferdinand, *received the death penalty* for his actions.
_____

11. Princip and his fellow conspirators were members of a terrorist society called the *Serbian Blade.*
_____

Name _____ Date _____

Draw a Poster

In the space below, make a recruiting poster urging young men to enlist in the armed forces of one of the nations mentioned in the chapter.

Use your imagination; give reasons why all able-bodied males should enlist and fight for their country. Make your poster attractive by using various colored pencils or crayons.

Name _____ Date _____

Distinguish between Complete Sentences or Fragments

Can you tell the difference between a complete sentence and a fragment? Fragments are statements that lack either a verb or a subject or do not express a complete thought. Fragments may be used in certain situations, but it is usually best to use complete sentences when writing.

Below is a group of statements relating to chapter 2. Some are fragments, while others are complete sentences. On the short line following each, write F if the statement is a fragment or S if it is a sentence. Then, on the long line below each statement that you mark as a fragment, rewrite the statement to make it a complete and true sentence.

1. Archduke Francis Ferdinand and his wife Sophie. _____

_____

2. Gavrilo Princip was a member of a terrorist group. _____

_____

3. Princip was unsuccessful in his attempts to kill himself. _____

_____

4. One month after the assassination of Archduke Francis Ferdinand. _____

_____

5. People standing in the crowd, cheering and waving flags. _____

_____

6. When soldiers marched off to war, convinced of an easy victory. _____

_____

7. Most people believed the war would be short. _____

_____

8. The Balkans, a region of great tension. _____

_____

Leaders in Wartime

Chapter 2 mentioned many of the leaders in Europe at the time of the war's start. However, a closer look at the personalities and peculiarities of a few is both worthwhile and interesting. Those covered in this chapter are not necessarily the most important or influential, but they certainly qualify as the most troubled and the most fascinating.

This is especially true of Nicholas II, the last czar of Russia. No leader was more unfit and unprepared to be the ruler of a nation than Nicholas. This was largely due to the fact that his stern, demanding father, Alexander III, saw him as weak and soft and did little to prepare him for the responsibilities of ruling the country. Although intelligent and well educated, Nicholas lacked common sense and was easily influenced by others. Perhaps this is what Kaiser Wilhelm II of Germany saw in Nicholas when he said that the czar was fit only to "live in a country house and raise turnips."

Czar Nicholas II of Russia escorting German visitors aboard ship prior to World War I.

Twenty-six-year-old Nicholas became czar in 1894 upon the death of his father. His reign could not have had a worst start. On the day of his coronation in 1895, thousands of people, many of them women and children, were trampled to death in an open field where they had gathered in anticipation of receiving the customary free gifts that were handed out on Coronation Day. Such gifts usually consisted of beer and enameled cups stamped with the imperial seal. A rumor began running through the crowd: There were not enough cups and beer to go around. This caused a mad rush toward the few loaded wagons that had arrived. In the process, countless people fell and were trampled underfoot. Although the new czar paid to have each of the dead buried in a separate coffin rather than a mass grave, Russians viewed the tragedy as a bad omen. It seemed that Nicholas's reign went nowhere but downhill from that point.

As Nicholas moved through his reign, it became apparent that perhaps Kaiser Wilhelm had been right: Had he not been born into royalty, the young czar might have been happy to "live in a country house and raise turnips." He loved his wife, Alexandra, deeply, and he was devoted to his five children. Nothing gave him more pleasure than spending time with his family. He particularly enjoyed simple things such as arranging pictures in the family

photo album. Any official duty that took him away from his family for a long time was painful.

As good-hearted as Nicholas was, nothing ever went right for him. In 1904, nine years after the Coronation Day disaster, he blundered into a war with Japan. Tiny Japan won, inflicting an embarrassing loss on the once-mighty Russia and opening the eyes of other nations to Russia's weakness.

In addition, Nicholas struggled at home with the illness of his only son, Alexis, who had been born with hemophilia, a disease that causes internal bleeding. Nicholas's wife, Alexandra, tirelessly pursued a cure for the boy. In doing so, she fell under the influence of an evil man named Rasputin. Rasputin, who called himself a monk, somehow had a hypnotic effect on the boy and was successful in stopping his bleeding. Through this power, he completely influenced the thoughts and actions of Czarina Alexandra, who in turn dominated Nicholas. The result was that Rasputin meddled in the affairs of the government. Russians were appalled that this unbathed "monk," who had a reputation for being a horse thief, village drunk, and woman chaser, had such influence over their royal family.

Nicholas was not a strong leader, and he chose weak advisors. This lack of leadership, combined with the amount of money it took to fight the war, soon crippled the Russian economy. Both soldiers at the front and people at home experienced severe shortages of food and fuel, and they blamed Nicholas. In March 1917, the Russian people revolted. Nicholas was forced to step down from his throne, and a new government was formed. This government negotiated a truce with the Central Powers.

Kaiser Wilhelm II of Germany was the direct opposite of Nicholas II. Whereas Nicholas was shy and gentle, Wilhelm was a bully and a braggart. Nicholas had never wanted to rule, while Wilhelm could hardly wait for his ailing father, Frederick III, to die. (Frederick III suffered from throat cancer and only ruled for three months.) While Nicholas loved quiet family life, Wilhelm relished parades and enjoyed going about in a spiked helmet, white cloak, and high black boots. Each morning a barber came to the palace to apply wax to the kaiser's mustache, which was bushy and turned up at the points.

Kaiser Wilhelm II liked to appear in military gear.

Wilhelm's abrasive personality may have been his reaction to living with a physical challenge. He was born with a withered left arm, the result of the surgeon who attended his birth nearly pulling the arm out of its socket with forceps. No amount of exercise and therapy in his youth caused the arm to grow normally. As a result, Wilhelm went to great lengths to conceal it. Every photograph of him shows his normal right arm concealing the hand of the deformed left one.

Because German rulers were expected to excel in physical activities, Wilhelm II drove himself to compensate for his arm. He became an excellent horseman and hunter. He also became a master swimmer, rower, and tennis player. Because he used his good arm exclusively, he developed an iron grip in his right hand. To further intimidate those who shook hands with him, he turned the rings on his right hand so that the stones faced up. All who shook his hand felt the sting of the stones bite into their own hands.

Franz Josef of Austria-Hungary was eighty-four years old at the outset of World War I.

Some historians place the blame for World War I on Wilhelm II. Seeking a place for Germany "in the sun," he built the German army into the strongest in Europe. He also increased the size of the navy until it was second only to that of Great Britain. Although he probably did not actively work to bring on the war, he did little to discourage it. When Austria-Hungary declared war on Serbia, he assured the Austrians that they could count on Germany's full support.

A third monarch ruling at the outbreak of World War I was Emperor Franz Joseph of Austria-Hungary. When the fighting started, he was eighty-four years old and had ruled for sixty-six years. This was longer than any monarch had ever sat on the throne of a nation.

During his long reign, Franz Joseph worked hard to be a good ruler. He kept the empire together, despite the ongoing unhappiness of the many different ethnic groups in his kingdom. His success was thanks in part to his wife Elizabeth. Affectionately called Sisi, she was a special favorite of the Hungarians. Elizabeth was very liberal-minded and no doubt influenced the emperor to grant a number of reforms within the empire.

Despite all of the good he did, Franz Joseph experienced more personal heartbreak during his reign than most other rulers. His long list of tragedies began in 1867 with the execution of his brother, Maximillian. In 1864 the French had installed him as emperor of Mexico, but three years later the Mexicans revolted and shot Maximillian.

Franz Joseph suffered another blow in 1889. His only son and heir to the throne, Crown Prince Rudolf, committed suicide along with his mistress. In 1896, Franz Joseph's younger brother, Karl Ludwig, died from drinking unclean water after a trip to the holy land. A year later, he suffered the worst tragedy of all. In 1897, his wife, Elizabeth, was assassinated by a knife-wielding Italian nationalist.

But that was not to be the end of it. Franz Joseph shipped his emotionally unstable younger brother, Archduke Viktor Ludwig, to the island of Capri because of unacceptable social behavior. Finally, in 1900, his nephew and heir, Archduke Francis Ferdinand, upset his uncle by marrying Sophie Chotek, a commoner. There seemed no end to Franz Joseph's problems.

Franz Joseph was a kindly man who had worked throughout his reign to keep the peace in Europe. But Austrian policy was strongly influenced by the man who was the Austrian army's chief of staff from late 1916 to late 1917, Field Marshal Franz Graf Conrad von Hötzendorf. Von Hötzendorf was what is commonly known as a "war hawk." This meant he favored war as a means of settling disagreements and grievances. In 1914 von Hötzendorf held Serbia directly responsible for the assassination of Francis Ferdinand in Bosnia. He saw the assassination as Serbia's attempt to undermine Austria-Hungary and free the slavic peoples then under Austrian rule. Serbia, he said, was "a dangerous little viper" and should be crushed.

As you have learned, Nicholas II, Wilhelm II, and Franz Joseph were troubled rulers in the years leading to World War I. Nicholas was faced with a crumbling empire on the verge of revolution. Wilhelm had territorial ambitions and wanted nothing better than to be a strong ruler like his grandfather, Wilhelm I. And Franz Joseph struggled with the problem of holding an empire together that consisted of many unhappy nationalities.

None of the three was around when the war ended. Nicholas and his family were executed by the Bolsheviks (communists) in July 1918. Wilhelm fled to the Netherlands at the end of the war. And Franz Joseph died in November 1916, two years before peace came.

Name _____ Date _____

Make a Cereal Box Report

Use an encyclopedia, Web site, or book about World War I to read about one of the leaders mentioned in this chapter. After completing your research, prepare a cereal box report for class.

Here Is What You Will Need:

1. An empty cereal box or any similar box
2. White paper (sheets of typing or printer paper will work best)
3. Glue or paste
4. A felt-tipped pen, or any pen suitable for drawing
5. Scissors

Here Is What You Do:

1. Glue or paste white paper over all of the sides of the box.
2. On the top edge of the box, write the name of the leader you have researched.
3. On one side panel, write the title or position that leader held.
4. On the other side panel, write the years the leader held that title or position.
5. On the front of the box, make a rough sketch of the leader.
6. On the back of the box, list two facts about the leader that were not mentioned in the chapter.

Give a brief report of your leader to the class.

Name _____ Date _____

Name Those Synonyms

Here is a list of twenty words taken from chapter 3. Write two synonyms for each on the lines provided. The way each word is used in the text is indicated by its part of speech in parentheses.

	Synonym	**Synonym**
1. major (adj)	_____	_____
2. stern (adj)	_____	_____
3. reign (n)	_____	_____
4. blundered (v)	_____	_____
5. inflicting (v)	_____	_____
6. dominated (v)	_____	_____
7. meddled (v)	_____	_____
8. conceal (v)	_____	_____
9. excel (v)	_____	_____
10. abrasive (adj)	_____	_____
11. intimidate (v)	_____	_____
12. discourage (v)	_____	_____
13. assured (v)	_____	_____
14. monarch (n)	_____	_____
15. tragedy (n)	_____	_____
16. revolted (v)	_____	_____
17. reform (n)	_____	_____
18. grievance (n)	_____	_____
19. anticipation (n)	_____	_____
20. customary (adj)	_____	_____

Name _____ Date _____

Compare Monarchs

You read about three European monarchs who were ruling when World War I broke out. Facts about each are listed opposite. To the left of each statement, write N if the statement refers to Nicholas II, W if it refers to Wilhelm II, or FJ if it refers to Franz Joseph.

1. _____ I was eighty-six years old when I died in 1916.

2. _____ I had a barber come to the palace every morning to wax my mustache.

3. _____ I sat on the throne longer than any ruling monarch.

4. _____ My country suffered a humiliating defeat at the hands of Japan in 1904–05.

5. _____ My arm was permanently injured during my birth.

6. _____ My coronation was marked by a disaster that resulted in thousands of people being trampled to death.

7. _____ I loved parades, and I enjoyed going about in a spiked helmet.

8. _____ My loving wife was assassinated by an Italian nationalist in 1897.

9. _____ I preferred spending time with my family to attending to the affairs of government.

10. _____ I was known as a braggart and a bully.

11. _____ My wife was known by the nickname of "Sisi."

12. _____ My son suffered from hemophilia.

13. _____ I stood by and let the evil monk Rasputin interfere in the affairs of my government.

14. _____ Franz Graf Conrad von Hötzendorf was the chief of staff of my army.

15. _____ I built my army into the strongest in Europe.

16. _____ My father did little to prepare me for the many responsibilities I would have when I ascended to the throne.

Name _____ Date _____

Convert Miles and Kilometers

Opposite are problems involving distances between five capital cities that played important roles in World War I. These cities were Vienna, Austria; Berlin, Germany; St. Petersburg, Russia; Paris, France; and London, England.

Solve the problems and write the correct answers on the blank lines. Space is provided for you to work each problem.

> **To convert miles to kilometers, multiply by 1.60934.**
> **To change kilometers to miles, divide by the same figure.**

1. The distance between Berlin, Germany, and Vienna, Austria, is 324 miles. This is _____ kilometers.

2. To travel from Vienna to St. Petersburg, Russia, one must cover 1,587 kilometers. Converted, this is _____ miles.

3. The distance from London, England, to Leningrad is 1,309 miles. This is equal to _____ kilometers.

4. It is a short distance from Paris, France, to London—only 343 kilometers. This is _____ miles.

5. A trip from Paris to St. Petersburg measures 1,350 miles. This is equal to _____ kilometers.

CHAPTER 4

New Methods of Warfare

World War I changed the way wars were fought. In previous years, columns of soldiers lined up in neat rows and advanced toward the enemy. Likewise, cavalrymen on horseback charged headlong into enemy lines, shouting and waving their sabers. However, both of these time-honored ways of fighting proved fruitless in 1914.

The first of these new weapons was the machine gun, which continues to fire as long as the trigger is pressed or until it runs out of bullets. An early machine gun first appeared in 1862 during the American Civil War. Invented by Richard Gatling, the Gatling gun was a multi-barreled weapon that the user fired by turning a crank. As he turned the crank, one barrel after another moved into firing position. After the Gatling gun's first use, many countries began using it.

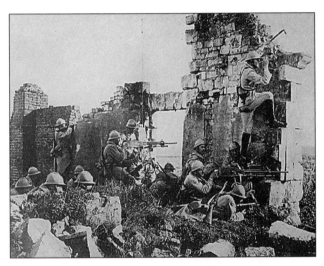

French troopers under General Gouraud drive back the Germans from the ruins of a cathedral near the Marne, 1918.

The first automatic machine gun appeared in 1884. It was invented by Hiram Maxim. In 1917, John Browning invented an improved gun. Like Gatling before them, Maxim and Browning were American inventors. The Maxim, Browning, and other types of machine guns were used during World War I.

The machine gun was a devastating weapon. It accounted for almost 90 percent of the war's casualties. It fired so many rounds so quickly that hundreds of advancing soldiers were slaughtered. Consequently, opposing sides dug long trenches across battlefronts and advanced very cautiously.

Another new weapon was the tank, which the British developed in 1915. To keep their new weapon a secret as long as possible, the British, while transporting the vehicles by train and ship, covered the weapons with canvas and labeled them "water tanks for Russia." This is how the tank got its name.

The British called their first tank Little Willie after the son of Kaiser Wilhelm. When they came out with an improved, larger model, they called it Big Willie. Big Willie could lumber along at the breathtaking speed of about 4 miles per hour! Big Willie was later called Mother, and after that similar models were called Mother's Children.

The first tanks did not see action until 1916. They were first used against the Germans in the Battle of the Somme, a river in northern France. How did the Germans react when they first saw the lumbering giants moving slowly toward them? To be sure, they were stunned. Many came out of their trenches and pointed. Others laughed. But when the metal monstrosities started spitting fire in their direction, they turned and ran.

As is true of many new innovations, the first tanks were not very effective. They were slow and cumbersome, and they ran out of gasoline too quickly. They also had a tendency to either break down or get stuck in mud. Of the 49 British tanks that were committed to the Battle of the Somme, only 18 actually took part. All the others developed mechanical problems or became mired in the muddy terrain. Even a year later, the tank's performance had improved little. At the Battle of Cambrai in 1917, 114 of 378 tanks broke down.

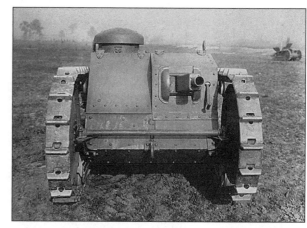

Front view of the two-man tank manufactured by the Ford Motor Company, Detroit, Michigan, ca. 1918.

Before the fighting ended in 1918, however, the tank had changed the way the war was fought. Troops no longer hunkered down in the trenches. The tank provided a means of protection and allowed troops to come out of the trenches and walk along or crouch behind it while advancing.

A third weapon used extensively for the first time during World War I was the airplane. The airplane was only about eleven years old when the fighting began, and it still resembled the Wright Brothers' box-kite design of 1903. Observers variously described it as either a "flying bird cage" or an "eggbeater." It was made almost entirely of wood, with its fuselage covered by cloth. As a result, once it was hit, it was relatively easy to bring down.

In 1914 few military men took the airplane seriously. Up to that point, it was seen as a novelty or toy for stunt pilots to thrill crowds with their acrobatics. When it did appear over the battlefield, it was used exclusively for observation and reconnaissance. Pilots flew over enemy positions and took photos of troop movements. They reported their findings back to headquarters, and no thought was given to using aircraft as combat weapons. When enemy pilots passed each other in the air, they usually nodded and waved and went about their business.

No one really knows when pilots became combatants. It has been suggested that the first might have stemmed from one pilot shouting insults at another as

they passed. What is known is that one day an angry pilot took a sack of bricks aloft with him and began throwing them at an enemy pilot. Matters quickly heated up after that.

From insults and bricks, pilots quickly graduated to pistols, rifles, and shotguns. Some even threw rusty chains into the open cockpits of enemy planes. Others dangled wires and chains from the underside of their aircraft in the hopes of entangling the enemy's propeller and causing a crash.

Sopwith F-1 "Camel"
USAF Museum

The Sopwith Camel, well-known to readers of the famous "Peanuts" cartoon strip, was the most successful fighter plane of WWI. Its pilots shot down more enemy aircraft than any other fighter of any of the warring nations.

Air combat became a reality when the Germans developed a machine gun that was synchronized to fire through propeller blades. Other countries soon did the same, and the air war began in earnest. The first pilot credited with bringing down an enemy aircraft was a Russian pilot named Petr Nesterov. On August 26, 1914, Nesterov succeeded in downing an Austrian plane flown by a Leutnant (Lieutenant) Baron von Rosenthal. But Nesterov did not shoot down von Rosenthal's plane. He rammed it in mid-air. Consequently, both planes plunged to the ground and both pilots were killed.

Four days after the war's first aircraft was destroyed, the first "air raid" of the conflict took place. On August 30, a German pilot named Lieutenant Ferdinand von Hiddessen flew over Paris and dropped five bombs over the side of his plane. One person below was killed, and several were injured. This act introduced the blackout to warfare. Afterward, towns and cities would douse their lights when enemy airplanes were detected nearby.

Each country produced aces—pilots who shot down at least five enemy planes. The top air ace of the war was Germany's Baron Manfred von Richthofen, who shot down eighty enemy aircraft. After the United States entered the war in 1917, Eddie Rickenbacker became the country's top ace. When the war ended a year later, he was credited with shooting down twenty-six enemy aircraft.

While soldiers had to endure the hardships of living in muddy trenches, airmen lived in comfortable quarters and enjoyed regular meals. But contrary to what one might think, soldiers on the ground did not envy the pilots above. Most thought: "It's a long way down and you only fall once."

A fourth new weapon of the war was poison gas. The Germans first used it to kill and demoralize as many soldiers in the trenches as possible. It did not, but it caused a lot of casualties. About 80,000 soldiers died from poison gas. Thirty percent of Americans who were killed in the war were victims of this horrible new weapon.

The first gas attack of the war occurred on April 22, 1915. French colonial troops in the trenches near the Belgian town of Ypres suddenly noticed a greenish-yellow cloud slowly moving toward their lines. The colorful cloud was chlorine gas. Many of the French soldiers were terrified and ran. Those who stayed all died from suffocation.

Other countries copied the Germans and started using poison gas. In addition to chlorine, the opposing sides used tear gas, phosgene, and mustard gas. Phosgene is a poisonous gas with a delayed effect. At first, its victim may feel ill but then seems to recover. In a few days however, phosgene causes acute inflammation of the lungs and brings on death.

Some sources say that mustard gas was the most deadly of all the gases used during World War I. Its name was derived from the fact that it smelled something like mustard. Mustard gas blistered the eyes, nose, throat, and skin and caused vomiting. Worse, it caused both internal and external bleeding and attacked the bronchial tubes. It was a slow killer, taking four or five weeks to kill its victim.

A final new innovation of the war were long-range guns. Perhaps the best known is Big Bertha. Big Bertha was named after the wife of German munitions maker Gustav Krupp. Big Bertha was so huge that it had to be transported by several large tractors and assembled where it would be used. Assembly took more than six hours and required a crew of 280 men. Big Bertha could hurl a 2,200-pound shell a distance of 9 miles. Other countries had long-range guns, but none could compare to Big Bertha.

As you can see, war drives people to develop new and more deadly weapons than those used in any previous war. The weapons developed during World War I were no exception.

Captain Edward Rickenbacker, America's premier "Ace," was officially credited with shooting down twenty-six enemy planes.

Name _____ Date _____

Make a Diary Entry

Pretend you are a German soldier taking part in the Battle of the Somme in France. Make a diary entry relating your thoughts and experiences as you look out from your trench and first catch sight of British tanks lumbering toward you.

Date _____

Dear Diary,

_____

_____

_____

_____

_____

_____

_____

_____

_____

_____

_____

_____

_____

_____

_____

_____

_____

_____

_____

Name _____ Date _____

Solve a New Weapons Puzzle

Fill in the sentences for clues to complete the puzzle about weapons that were used extensively for the first time during World War I.

1. _ _ _ _ _ N _
2. _ E _ _ _ _
3. W _ _ _ _
4. W _ _ _ _ _
5. _ _ _ _ _ E _ _ _ _ _ _ _
6. _ _ _ A _
7. _ _ P _ _ _ _
8. _ _ _ O _ _
9. _ _ N _ _
10. _ _ _ S

From *Everyday Life: World War I* © Good Year Books. This page may be reproduced for classroom use only by the actual purchaser of the book. www.goodyearbooks.com

1. The _____ were the first to use poison gas.

2. Germany developed a long-range gun called Big _____.

3. The British disguised their tanks as _____ containers.

4. The first tank to be produced was called Little _____.

5. The United States' leading ace of World War I was Eddie _____.

6. _____ Maxim invented the first automatic machine gun.

7. Phosgene is an example of a _____ gas.

8. The Germans used _____ gas at Ypres in Belgium.

9. The Battle of the Somme was fought in northern _____.

10. The use of machine _____ led to the war in western Europe bogging down into trench warfare.

Name _____ Date _____

Use Context Clues to Complete Sentences

Here is a brief account of new methods of warfare that characterized World War I. Fill in the blanks in the sentences of the story using the words provided.

bogged

cause

charges

combat

deadliest

different

escaping

fire

galloping

horrible

minutes

mustard

soldiers

staggering

user

weapon

World War I was a _____ kind of war. Gone were the days when _____ advanced across open fields to do _____ with the enemy. Also gone were the cavalry _____ of old, with men on horseback _____ to what they hoped would be glory. Instead, fighting in World War I _____ down into trench warfare. The primary _____ of this was the introduction of the machine gun.

A machine gun could _____ a steady stream of bullets as long as the _____ pressed on the trigger. The result was _____. Attacking troops were mowed down by the hundreds in a matter of _____. To escape such slaughter, each side hid in trenches they dug deep into the ground.

Poison gas was another new _____ of World War I. Before gas masks were introduced, soldiers had no way of _____ the deadly fumes that suddenly descended upon them. Perhaps the worst of all the gases was _____ gas. This gas caused _____ suffering before its victim finally died.

The machine gun and poison gas were the _____ of the new weapons used in World War I.

Name _____ Date _____

Create a Bar Graph of Your Own

When World War I began, airplanes had only been around for eleven years. As a result, countries began the war with a small number of aircraft. Listed here, according to some sources, are the actual numbers of airplanes five of the countries possessed.

Use these figures and create your own bar graph in the space below.

France 260
Russia 100
Germany 46
Great Britain 29
Italy 26

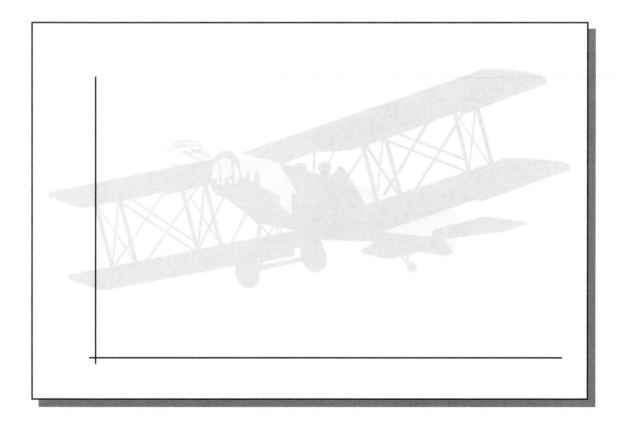

CHAPTER 5

Life in the Trenches

Remember that almost everyone in Europe expected the war to be short. Many thought it would be simple and easily won. Few people thought it would last more than a couple of months, and fewer still would have believed it would last four years. And absolutely no one could foresee that the conflict would bog down into a slugfest fought from trenches.

When the war began, the Germans were ready with a plan of action called the Schlieffen Plan, which was named for Count Alfred von Schlieffen, the chief of staff of the German army until 1906. Looking ahead, von Schlieffen had devised a plan that called for the German army to attack France through Belgium. Some German troops would keep the French busy along the German–French border, while the bulk of German forces would swing down through Belgium and cut off the French from the rear. Germany wanted to knock France out of the war before Russia could get her troops ready to fight.

Germans in their well-protected trenches on the Belgian frontier taking aim at their enemy.

In the first months of the war, the Germans advanced through Belgium to within 30 miles of Paris. If the Germans had been successful in taking Paris, the war might have ended then and there. But as the Germans advanced, French soldiers arrived at the front in hundreds of taxicabs. They stopped the Germans at the Marne River. Their arrival helped determine the outcome of the battle.

This First Battle of the Marne was fought from about September 5 to September 10, 1914 (sources differ on exact dates). The battle resulted in a victory of sorts for the French and the British. Although they did not inflict a real defeat on the Germans, they at least stopped the Germans from proceeding on to Paris.

Not wanting to lose the territory they had gained, the Germans dug trenches at the farthest point of their advance into France. This line of trenches became known as the *western front*. The French and the British soon dug trenches facing those of the Germans. Eventually, zigzag lines of trenches stretched from the North Sea to Switzerland. This was a distance of 440 miles.

The zigzag pattern was designed to prevent the enemy from lobbing shells in a straight line and wiping out large numbers of troops at one time.

In general, there were four lines of trenches. The closest to the enemy was the front-line trench. This was the trench where most of the fighting took place. Soldiers on both sides usually spent about a week in the front-line trench. Then they were rotated back to one of the other trenches.

Behind the front-line trench were the support, reserve, and communication trenches. Troops in support and reserve were on standby and had to be ready at any moment to move ahead to the front-line trench. All movement of troops and supplies was coordinated from the communication trench.

To prevent easy access to their trenches, both sides strung barbed wire all along the length of their dugouts. Sometimes soldiers embedded razor blades and tin cans in the wire to make cutting and getting through it even more difficult. The area between the enemies' barbed wire and trenches was called *No Man's Land*. No Man's was often measured in mere yards. "Over the top" was the signal for troops to climb out of the trench and charge into No Man's Land. This contested territory between the trenches was nothing more than a killing field. As troops tried to advance, they were mowed down by murderous machine gun fire.

U.S. Food Administration drawing of a soldier charging through barbed wire, ca. 1917.

Machine gun fire and shells lobbed at regular intervals into the trenches cost the lives of thousands of soldiers each day. One source states that on any given day, almost 2,500 troops were killed. Another 9,000 were wounded and 1,100 declared missing. The latter usually meant that the missing soldiers' bodies were so badly damaged that identification was impossible. All together, possibly one-third of the casualties in World War I occurred in the trenches. At the 1916 Battle of the Somme alone, the British are said to have lost 20,000 men on the very first day.

Machine gun fire and incoming artillery shells were not the only horrors faced by men in the trenches. There was also poison gas. You have already learned that both sides used chlorine, phosgene, mustard, and other gases. Armies quickly distributed gas masks, but early models left much to be desired. They included pads soaked in horse urine, which was supposed to neutralize

the effects of the gas. It is easy to understand why some men preferred to use handkerchiefs and wet rags instead.

In addition to these horrors, the trench soldier of World War I had to cope with millions of rats. Rats were attracted to the trenches by the smell of empty food cans and dead bodies. Some rats grew to the size of cats. It was not uncommon for rats to start gnawing on the bodies of wounded men who couldn't defend themselves. Rats became so bold that they would filch food from the pockets of sleeping men. Many troops were awakened by rats crawling across their faces. One British soldier related how he was awakened by a rat that had gnawed through his clothes and had started biting his hip!

Soldiers fought back as best they could with bayonets and rifles. Rats were shot, stabbed, and clubbed to death. But efforts to eliminate them proved futile. A single rat couple could produce up to 900 offspring a year.

Another problem associated with life in the trenches was lice. Lice not only made men miserable; they caused trench fever. While not deadly, trench fever could take a soldier out of action for days. No amount of hot baths and delousing in rest areas could kill all the lice eggs. Some managed to survive even after a soldier's grimy uniform was washed.

As though rats, lice, and gunfire were not enough, soldiers in the front trenches also had to deal with trench foot, a fungal infection. Soldiers contracted it by standing in trenches that were constantly flooded. One soldier stated that anyone who suffered from trench foot might see his feet swell to two to three times their normal size. In such cases, he said, one could stick them with a bayonet and not feel a thing. Trench foot could lead to gangrene, resulting in the amputation of a person's foot—or feet.

The British and the French suffered more from trench foot than the Germans. When trench warfare first began, the Germans claimed the best sites and dug their trenches on high ground. This left the British and the French with no place to dig but in low-lying areas, so their trenches often flooded when it rained. Men spent days standing in mud and water. Many contracted trench foot. Others fared even worse. It was not uncommon for a wounded man to fall in the muddy water and drown.

What with all the horrors associated with trench warfare, some men simply broke down. The constant shelling and firing caused what is known as "shell shock." Some men became psychologically paralyzed. Others developed muscle contractions. Still others went temporarily deaf or blind. Some could not stand the shelling any longer and committed suicide. Some ran away, only to be shot

as deserters when found. More than one stuck his head above the trenches and welcomed being shot by a sniper. Because there was nothing wrong with these men physically, unsympathetic officers and doctors labeled them cowards and malingerers. (A malingerer is someone pretending to be sick.)

Life in the trenches went far to take the glamour and excitement out of going to war. How many young men do you think would have rushed to recruitment offices in 1914 had they known they would spend four years fighting out of muddy trenches? Very few, most likely.

Some underage boys, looking to see the world or escape strict parents, managed to get into the army. One young British soldier related that when he told the recruitment officer he was only sixteen, the officer replied, "Well, son, go back out, come back in, and tell me your age again." The young boy went out, returned, and told the officer he was nineteen. At that he was accepted, and he became a soldier. One boy in the British army was thirteen. Still another was only twelve. In their eagerness to attract recruits, armies were rather lax in trying to determine the age of young boys who wanted to enlist.

For four long years the opposing armies faced each other in the trenches. For four long years men died, seemingly for no reason. One day they would go "over the top" and perhaps gain a few yards of the enemy's territory. The next day they would be driven back to their original position. This was pretty much the story for most of the war. The stalemate brought about by trench warfare did not end until the United States entered the fighting in 1917. The addition of American troops enabled the Allies to drive back the Germans and bring an end to the war.

French soldier resting in a trench after a battle.

Name _____ Date _____

Compare and Contrast Wars

World War I was different from wars fought in the past. Likewise, it was different from wars that have been fought in modern times. With this in mind, write your best answers to the questions.

1. Explain how World War I was unlike any previous war.

_____

_____

_____

_____

_____

_____

_____

2. Explain how World War I was different from wars today.

_____

_____

_____

_____

_____

_____

_____

3. Why do you think people saw World War I as the "war to end all wars"?

_____

_____

_____

_____

_____

_____

From *Everyday Life: World War I* © Good Year Books. This page may be reproduced for classroom use only by the actual purchaser of the book. www.goodyearbooks.com

Name _____ Date _____

Conduct an Interview

Pretend you are a reporter for a European newspaper. It is the year 1915, and a soldier who was wounded in the trenches has returned home to recover.

Write a newspaper interview of your conversation with the wounded soldier. Think of questions to ask and his possible responses. Be sure to give your interview a title.

Title of your story

_____

_____

_____

_____

_____

_____

_____

_____

_____

_____

_____

_____

_____

_____

_____

_____

_____

_____

_____

_____

_____

_____

_____

_____

Name _____ Date _____

Recall Information You Have Read

Without looking back over the chapter, see how many of the following questions you can answer.

1. What was the Schlieffen Plan?
   _____
   _____

2. At which battle was the German drive to take Paris halted?
   _____

3. Where was No Man's Land?
   _____
   _____

4. What did it mean to "go over the top"?
   _____
   _____

5. Why were German trenches preferable to those of the French and the British?
   _____
   _____

6. What caused trench fever?
   _____
   _____

7. What was trench foot? What caused it? What did it often lead to?
   _____
   _____

8. What opinion did officers and doctors have of soldiers who suffered from shell shock?
   _____
   _____

9. Why were rats such a problem in the trenches?
   _____
   _____

10. Why were trenches dug in zigzag fashion?
    _____
    _____

Name _____   Date _____

Write a Persuasive Essay

In chapter 5 you read about the horrors experienced by soldiers in World War I. What is your opinion of war? In general, there are several positions people hold regarding war.

They are:

1. War is never justified and should be avoided at all costs.

2. War is justified only if a nation is first attacked by another nation.

3. Sometimes a preemptive war is necessary. This means a nation must be the aggressor and attack another it fears poses a threat to its security.

Choose one of these three positions and write a persuasive essay on the lines provided. Give arguments supporting the way you feel.

_____

_____

_____

_____

_____

_____

_____

_____

_____

_____

_____

_____

_____

_____

_____

CHAPTER 6

Major Battles

orld War I started out in traditional fashion. Troops were on the move and territorial gains were made. Following the Schlieffen Plan, the Germans invaded Belgium on August 3, 1914. Belgium was a neutral country (it did not take sides), but this meant little to the Germans. They easily swept the Belgian army aside and got within 30 miles of Paris.

With the German army fast approaching, the French government made plans to move their offices to Bordeaux, far to the southeast. Throughout Paris, citizens hurried to prepare for what they considered the inevitable. But they were determined to hold out. They dug trenches fortified by logs, mounds of earth, and barbed wire on the outskirts of the city. They made plans to blow up buildings and bridges to slow down the Germans. And they stored bread and other foods to sustain the people during the attack.

Then several miracles occurred that saved Paris. First, General Joseph-Simon Gallieni, who was entrusted with the city's defense, rounded up buses and some six hundred taxicabs and rushed six thousand reserve troops to the Marne River. As you read in chapter 5, their arrival helped stop the German advance. Second, General Ferdinand Foch, who commanded the French Ninth Army, decided to launch a counterattack. His troops, along with the British, opened a gap in the German lines. The Germans retreated and fell back to the Aisne River to the northeast. There they dug in, and four years of trench warfare in western Europe began.

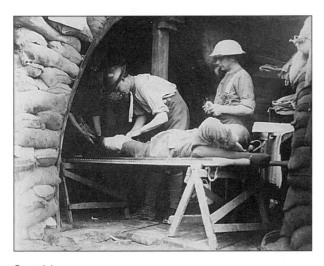

Scottish soldiers being examined in a dressing station on the British Western Front, 1914.

General Foch's counterattack of the Germans began what was called the First Battle of the Marne. Fought from September 5–10, 1914, it marked the first bloody battle of the war. Sources differ as to the number of troops lost, but some say that the French suffered about 250,000 casualties. The British, with far fewer troops, had some 12,700 casualties. German policy did not allow an announcement of their losses, but it is believed their casualties equaled those of the French.

Another major battle was the Battle of Tannenberg. It was important because it came close to knocking Russia out of the war early. After this battle, the Russians would never pose a serious threat to the Central Powers.

From *Everyday Life: World War I* © Good Year Books. This page may be reproduced for classroom use only by the actual purchaser of the book. www.goodyearbooks.com

Tannenberg was a village in East Prussia in the northeastern part of Germany. It became the site of a heated battle between the Russians and the Germans from August 27–30, 1914. Aware that the Germans were advancing through Belgium toward Paris in late August, France urged the Russians to attack German positions in East Prussia. Such an attack would force Germany to fight a war on two fronts—the western front in France and the eastern front in Prussia. It would also hopefully help relieve the pressure on Paris.

Remember that the Russian army was woefully unprepared and backward. Its only strength lay in its sheer numbers—it included some six million troops. But many of these troops did not even possess a weapon. Some estimates place the number of Russian soldiers without rifles as high as one-third of the army. They were ordered into battle anyway, told to pick up the rifles of their comrades who were shot and killed. One source even states that Russian soldiers once attacked a machine gun nest armed only with ax handles.

In late August 1914, the Russians, led by General Alexandr Samsonov, attacked German positions at Tannenberg. In four days, the Russians suffered some 50,000 killed or wounded. Another 92,000 were taken prisoner. By comparison, the Germans lost only about 20,000 troops. General Samsonov was so distraught that he shot himself. Two weeks later, Russia was defeated again, in the Battle of the Masurian Lakes. This time the Russians lost about 100,000 men. Another 30,000 were taken prisoner. Russia was no longer a threat to the Germans.

The Battle of Verdun in 1916 was another major battle. It lasted ten months, beginning on February 21, 1916, and continuing until December 19 of that year. Two million men were involved, and almost half of these became casualties. Estimates of the number killed on both sides vary widely. Some sources say the French lost 163,000 men and the Germans 143,000. Others sources place the numbers much higher, with the French counting 315,000 killed and the Germans 282,000. Except for the fact that it became a symbol of French resistance, little was gained from the bloody battle at Verdun.

As you already know, the Battle of the Somme in northwestern France was the first battle in which tanks were used. The battle began on July 1, 1916, and continued until November 18. For a full week before the British attack, Allied forces subjected the German trenches to a continuous barrage of artillery bombardment. The British were confident that the barrage had killed many of the German defenders. They were wrong. No sooner had British troops gone "over the top" on the morning of July 1 than they came under heavy artillery

and machine gun fire. Many never made it out of the trenches. Of the 100,000 who did, almost 20,000 were killed before they reached the German position.

That first charge by the British at the Battle of the Somme lasted only thirty minutes. A British general, safe in his position in the rear, commented: "It was a magnificent display of trained and disciplined valour (valor), and its assault only failed of success because dead men can advance no farther." It may have been a "magnificent display" in the eyes of one officer, but it achieved little. In more than three months of fighting, the British had gained only 10 kilometers of ground—and that at the cost of more than 400,000 casualties.

The Battle of Cambrai was fought in northern France from November 20 to December 3, 1917. Like most battles on the western front, it accomplished little, except to cause more casualties. It did, however, seem to prove two points. First, no artillery bombardment preceded the attack. This allowed the British and the French an element of some surprise. Instead of artillery, two hundred tanks charged at the German trenches. Too many broke down to have much effect on the outcome, but the tank did allow troops to come out of the trenches and advance toward the enemy with some protection from murderous machine gun fire. This second point would become important later in the war.

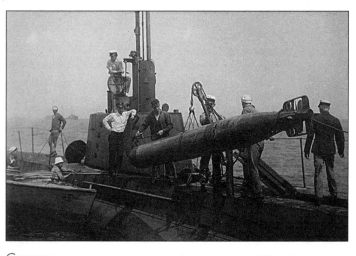

German submarine crew recovering a torpedo, ca. 1918

The naval Battle of Jutland, the only major naval engagement of the entire war, was fought off the coast of Denmark from May 31 to June 1, 1916. Jutland is the peninsula on which Denmark is located. Prior to this date, battles between opposing ships had been limited to blockades and submarine activity. A blockade is the practice of ships preventing supplies from entering enemy ports. The British policy was to starve Germany out of the war by stopping shipments of food to Germany. In hopes of breaking the blockade, the Germans resorted to submarine warfare. They announced that they would sink any ship that came close to the British Isles.

On May 31, 1916, the German fleet in the Baltic sailed out to challenge the British fleet. The British welcomed the challenge. Although German ships were superior and their firepower more accurate, the British had the advantage in sheer numbers. They could lose more ships and still come out the winner.

And that is what happened. In a battle fought into the night, the British lost fourteen ships, but in the process they sank eleven of those of the Germans.

By the spring of 1917, Germany's continuation of submarine warfare finally brought the United States into the war. On April 2, President Woodrow Wilson asked Congress to declare war on Germany. They complied, and war was later declared on the other members of the Central Powers as well. The entrance of the United States into the war turned the tide in favor of the Allies.

American soldiers and marines fought several important battles in northern France. At Château-Thierry, U.S. Army troops drove the Germans back across the Marne, where they had attempted another major offensive. Then a brigade of American marines won an important battle in Belleau Wood on the road to Paris. Both of these battles took place in June 1918.

The battles against the Germans in northern France produced America's first true hero. His name was Alvin York, and he was a reluctant soldier from Tennessee. Because of his religious beliefs, York did not believe in killing another human being. When he received his draft notice from the army, he wrote something on it like "Don't want to go," and mailed it back. He soon learned, however, that he had no choice in the matter. In June, he found himself on a troop ship bound for France.

On October 8, 1918, in the Argonne Forest of northern France, Alvin York performed the deed that made him an American hero. On that day, he almost single-handedly killed the crew of a German machine gun nest and captured 132 other soldiers. At the height of the fighting, he "tetched off" 6 Germans coming directly toward him with fixed bayonets. "Tetched off" was Tennessee hill talk for "picked off." York later explained that he shot the sixth man in line first, and then proceeded to "tetch off" numbers 5, 4, 3, 2, and 1 in that order. He said that by firing in such a manner, those in front never knew those behind them were falling. This feat caused a German major to yell that he would surrender all of his men if York would stop shooting—and that is how Alvin York came to capture 132 German soldiers.

In a little more than a month after York's heroics, Germany surrendered, and World War I came to an end.

Sergeant Alvin C. York, 328th Infantry, who with the aid of 17 men captured 132 German prisoners. He is shown here on the hill on which the raid took place October 8, 1918, in the Argonne Forest, near Cornay, France.

Name _____ Date _____

Solve a Battle Puzzle

ACROSS

5 Battle fought in East Prussia

6 Country whose submarine warfare brought the United States into the war

7 French general at the Battle of the Marne

8 Country located on the Jutland peninsula

11 French city the Germans hoped to take

12 Only major naval battle of the war

13 Battle in which 200 tanks were used

14 Battle in which tanks were first used

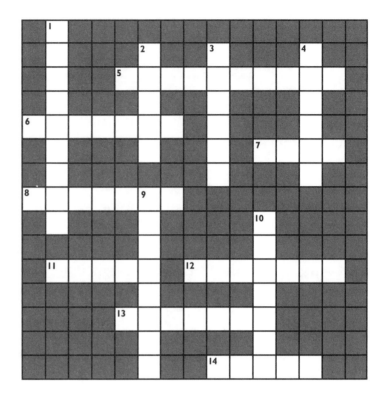

DOWN

1 Alvin York was from this state.

2 Battle where the German advance into France was stopped

3 Battle that lasted ten months

4 The Argonne is in this country.

9 They lost the Battle of Tannenberg.

10 Neutral country invaded by Germany in 1914

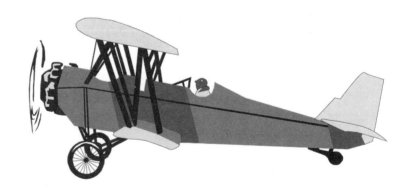

From Everyday Life: World War I *© Good Year Books. This page may be reproduced for classroom use only by the actual purchaser of the book. www.goodyearbooks.com*

Name _____   Date _____

Solve Four Word Problems

In the spaces provided, solve these word problems dealing with the battles of World War I.

1. At the Battle of Tannenberg, the Russians suffered 142,000 casualties. Of this number, about 50,000 were killed. What percent of the total casualties does 50,000 represent?

    _____ Answer

2. You read that some 600 taxicabs and an undetermined number of buses carried 6,000 French reserve troops to the Marne in September 1914. If 5 soldiers rode in each taxi, how many were transported by bus?

    _____ Answer

3. The Battle of the Somme was fought from July 1 to November 18, 1916. In round numbers, how many weeks did the battle last?

    _____ Answer

4. Twenty-five ships were sunk at the naval Battle of Jutland. The British lost 14, while the Germans lost 11. What percent of the total number of ships sunk were British?

    _____ Answer

Name _____ Date _____

Use Your Critical Thinking Skills

Think about the questions presented to you on this page. Then write your best answer for each on the lines provided.

Alvin York was reluctant to go to war because he was a conscientious objector.

A conscientious objector is a person who does not believe in taking up arms against others. York's reason for not wanting to go to war stemmed from his religious beliefs. He simply believed it was wrong to kill another person.

With this in mind, answer the following questions.

1. Should a person be exempt (excused) from going to war because of religious beliefs? Why or why not?

_____

_____

_____

_____

_____

2. Tell why or why not you think the following people should be exempt from military service:

a. a married person with children

_____

_____

_____

_____

b. a college student

_____

_____

_____

c. a person with a physical impairment

_____

_____

_____

_____

_____

Name _____ Date _____

Draw and Label a Map of France

During World War I, almost all the fighting on the western front took place in France. Soldiers on both sides became familiar with such places as Paris, Verdun, the Somme, the Marne, and the Aisne. How familiar are you with some of these French locations?

Using an atlas or an encyclopedia as a guide, draw a rough map of France. On your map, label the cities of Paris, Verdun, Cambrai, and Bordeaux. Also draw in and label these rivers: the Marne, the Somme, and the Aisne. Use the space below to draw your map.

CHAPTER 7

The United States Enters the War

On February 4, 1915, Germany declared that the waters surrounding the British Isles would from that day on be a war zone. This meant that their U-boats (submarines) would sink any ship trying to carry supplies to the British. Their action was in response to the British navy blockading their home ports. Little did the Germans realize at the time that they had set in motion a chain of events that would bring the United States into the war on the side of the Allies.

A drawing of the R.M.S. *Lusitania* as a second torpedo hits behind a gaping hole in the hull.

Although the United States was determined to stay out of the war when it began in 1914, certain actions on the part of the Germans slowly turned American opinion against the Central Powers. The sinking of the British passenger ship *Lusitania* by a German U-boat was the first such action.

The *Lusitania* was a large ocean liner that had been sailing between England and the United States since 1907. On May 7, 1915, it was sunk 10 miles off the coast of Ireland. The Germans claimed that the liner was carrying munitions bound for England. The British denied this claim and called the German act "murder on the high seas."

Was the *Lusitania* carrying munitions at the time she was sunk? From the start, there was evidence that she was. The captain of the U-boat that sank the huge ship, Walter Schwieger, later stated that he only fired one torpedo at the vessel. But there were two explosions. The second explosion was tremendous, and it was this explosion that brought the ship down. The British claimed that this second explosion might have been the result of coal dust. The Germans stated they believed it was caused by munitions stored in the hold of the ship.

There were 1,924 passengers aboard the *Lusitania*. Only 726 survived. Exactly 1,198 perished. This number included somewhere between 114 and 128 Americans. Almost every source gives a different number. Regardless, none, according to the Germans, would have died had they heeded the warning of the German Embassy in Washington, D.C.

Before the *Lusitania* sailed from New York on May 1, the German ambassador had issued a warning in the newspapers. The warning advised

Americans that it was unwise to travel on ships carrying supplies to England. Undoubtedly passengers thought the *Lusitania* carried no supplies. They were wrong, and much later it was learned that the ship indeed carried munitions in its hold.

The sinking of the *Lusitania* brought a stern warning from President Wilson to the Germans. He informed the German government that the United States would not tolerate another attack on its citizens. Not wanting to draw the United States into the war, the Germans backed down. For the next two years, they limited their submarine activity in the Atlantic. But in 1917, they resumed their attacks on any ship bound for the British Isles. They claimed this was necessary because of the effect of the British blockade of their own ports. This resumption of German submarine warfare finally brought the United States into the war.

Propaganda also played a part in turning American opinion against the Germans. Posters compared the Germans to the Huns, a fierce Asiatic tribe that once threatened all of Europe. Pictures showed beastly-looking German soldiers in Belgium killing babies and assaulting women. Many tales of atrocities (cruel and brutal acts) were exaggerated, but just as many were true. In some Belgian towns, all the citizens were rounded up and assembled in the main square. Every tenth person or every second person (or whatever) was singled out and lined up in columns. Then they were marched to an empty lot or field and shot. Men, women, children, and priests were shot. No one was exempt. In one town, a German firing squad shot and killed a three-week-old infant!

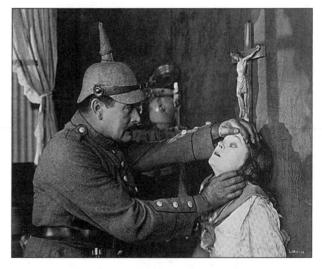

Mae Marsh, as a Belgian girl and A. C. Gibbons as a German soldier in Goldwyn's motion picture *Stake Uncle Sam to Play Your Hand,* 1918.

Why were the Germans so brutal against innocent people? Some sources state that their behavior was well planned in advance of their invasion. Others believed the atrocities were a direct result of unexpected resistance on the part of the Belgian civilian population. Belgians cut telephone and telegraph lines and blew up railroads and bridges. Every Belgian citizen was seen as a possible sniper or saboteur. (A saboteur is someone who intentionally damages property.) In the Germans' view, a few people randomly shot and their homes burned might go far to discourage such activities. These acts of brutality slowly turned world opinion against the Germans.

A final factor that brought the United States into the war was the Zimmerman Telegram. This was a note sent by the Germany's Foreign Minister to German embassies in Washington and Mexico. The note instructed the German ambassador in Mexico to approach the Mexican government about declaring war on the United States. Germany was almost certain that once she renewed unrestricted submarine warfare, the United States would enter the war, and an attack by the Mexicans would keep American troops occupied far away from Europe.

The Zimmerman Telegram was intercepted by British Secret Service agents and turned over to President Wilson. Needless to say, the president was furious. The contents of the telegram were unbelievable. If Mexico joined the Central Powers and declared war on the United States, she would be rewarded with the return of Texas, Arizona, and New Mexico. These were states that had been formed from territory seized from Mexico after the Mexican War in 1848. Now Germany was promising these lands back to the Mexicans.

A soldier of the 71st Regiment Infantry, New York National Guard, saying good-bye to his sweetheart as his regiment leaves for Camp Wadsworth, Spartanburg, South Carolina, 1917.

President Wilson made the Zimmerman Telegram public on February 23, 1917. Americans were both shocked and enraged when they learned what it proposed. After striving for three years to keep the United States neutral, President Wilson asked Congress to declare war on Germany. Congress complied on April 6. Three years of simply watching the terrible slaughter in Europe soon came to an end. Congress' declaration of war had now made the United States a part of it.

With the United States officially in the war, the U.S. government began to increase the size of the nation's armed forces. In 1917 the army consisted of under 200,000 troops. Some sources maintain the number was as low as 110,000. Many more were needed if the United States was to make an impact.

A call went out for volunteers. Many responded, but their numbers were too small to form an adequate fighting force. On May 18, Congress passed the Selective Service Act. This law required all men ages twenty-one to thirty to register for a draft. These ages were later extended to men eighteen to forty-five. Altogether, 23.9 million men registered. Of this number, about 2.8 million were actually inducted, or taken into the armed forces. Their names were chosen by lottery. In 1917 and 1918, about one million of the men called up saw service in France.

Americans who sailed for France in 1917 made up what was called the American Expeditionary Force. This force was commanded by General John J. Pershing. Pershing was called to his new post from his campaign along the Mexican-American border. Mexico was in the midst of a revolution, and American troops were sent to Texas to protect Americans who lived along the Rio Grande River. While in the southwest, Pershing suffered a tragedy that might have completely crushed a weaker person. On August 27, 1915, a fire destroyed his family's home in San Francisco. His wife Helen and their three daughters died in the blaze. Only their son Warren survived. People everywhere were touched by Pershing's loss. Even Pancho Villa, the notorious Mexican rebel he would later chase, sent his condolences.

American foot soldiers who were sent to France to fight were called *doughboys.* The exact origin of that name is not known. There are two theories. One states that the term originated in the 1850s when soldiers cleaned their belts with a "dough" made of clay. The other holds that the name stemmed from the 1860s when the large buttons on army uniforms were said to resemble "doughboys,"

Bayonet practice, Camp Bowie, Fort Worth, Texas, ca. 1918.

bread dough that was rolled thin and deep-fried.

You read in the previous chapter that the arrival of American troops in France turned the tide of war in favor of the Allies. You also read about the major battles in which the Americans took part, and of the heroic exploits of Sergeant Alvin York. But other Americans distinguished themselves as well. These included soldiers of the all-African-American 369th Infantry Regiment.

The 369th Infantry Regiment spent more than six months in the trenches of France. During that time, they lost almost half their number. They fought so well and so fiercely that the Germans called them the "Hell Fighters." Exactly 171 members of the regiment received the Croix de Guerre, France's highest military medal.

The United States paid a high price for getting involved in World War I. Of the two million American soldiers who fought in World War I, about 126,000 were killed. More than 200,000 were wounded, and 4,500 either taken prisoner or declared missing.

Name _____ Date _____

Interpret Patriotic Verses

As you have learned, Americans wanted no part of World War I when it began in 1914. Most were of the opinion that the war was a European affair and was therefore no concern of theirs. Early American war songs reflected this view. One popular song of 1915 was entitled "Don't Take My Darling Boy Away." The picture on the front of the sheet music shows a mother on her knees begging what appears to be a recruiting officer not to take her son away to war.

By 1917 American opinion had come full circle. After President Woodrow Wilson asked Congress to declare war on April 6 of that year, a number of patriotic songs appeared. Verses from two of these songs, "America, Here's My Boy" and "Over There" appear here. Write your best answers to the questions concerning each.

1. Part of "America, Here's My Boy" includes the following lyrics: "America, he is my only one; My hope, my pride and joy/But if I had another, he would march beside his brother/America here's my boy." What view does the mother of this young man have toward the war?

_____

_____

_____

_____

_____

2. Four lines from "Over There" read: "Make your daddy glad/To have had such a lad." and "Make your mother proud of you/And the old Red, White, and Blue." What do these lines urge a young man to do?

_____

_____

_____

_____

_____

3. In the chorus of "Over There," the song ends with the lines: "We'll be over, we're coming over/And we won't come back till it's over, over there." What do these lines tell about Americans' attitude in 1917?

_____

_____

_____

_____

_____

Name _____ Date _____

Write a Story for *The Smallville Times*

Pretend that you are a reporter for *The Smallville Times*. The year is 1917, and the United States has just entered the war. Your assignment is to write a story about Tom Hawkins, the first young man in your town to volunteer for the army.

On the lines provided, write the lead paragraph to your story. Be sure to include answers to the five "W" questions (Who? What? When? Where? and Why?) that are characteristic of a good lead paragraph. The headline has been written for you.

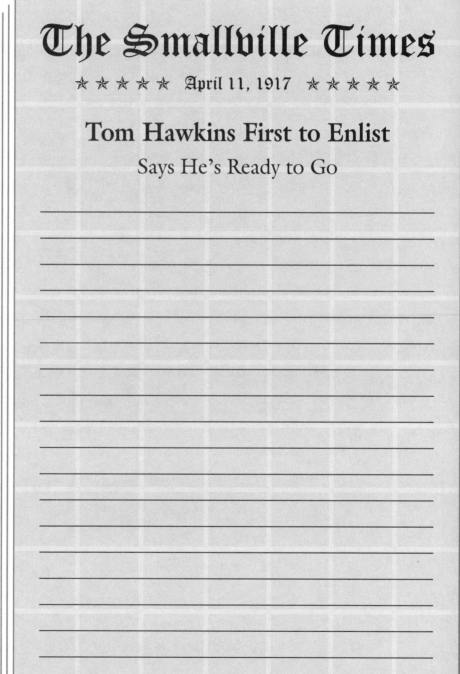

The Smallville Times

✶ ✶ ✶ ✶ April 11, 1917 ✶ ✶ ✶ ✶ ✶

Tom Hawkins First to Enlist
Says He's Ready to Go

_____

_____

_____

_____

_____

_____

_____

_____

_____

_____

_____

_____

_____

_____

_____

_____

_____

Name _____ Date _____

Distinguish between Fact and Opinion

Some of the statements on this page are facts; others are only opinions. Put an F on the line before each statement you think is a fact and an O before each statement you think is an opinion.

1. _____ It would have been in the best interest of the United States to have remained neutral during World War I.

2. _____ Allied propaganda played a role in bringing the United States into the war.

3. _____ The Allies would have eventually won the war regardless of what action the United States took.

4. _____ The Germans were justified in sinking the *Lusitania* without warning.

5. _____ It was later proven that the *Lusitania* was carrying munitions.

6. _____ A stern warning from the United States following the sinking of the *Lusitania* caused Germany to suspend its U-boat activity for awhile.

7. _____ The Germans proved to be the most brutal invaders of all time.

8. _____ Had it not been for the Zimmerman Telegram, the United States would have never joined the Allies in World War I.

9. _____ The Zimmerman Telegram was first intercepted by the British Secret Service.

10. _____ The Central Powers would have won the war had Mexico joined forces with them.

11. _____ Gen. John J. Pershing was the greatest military commander the United States has ever produced.

12. _____ The addition of the American Expeditionary Force to the western front helped turn the tide against the Central Powers.

13. _____ The all-African-American 369th Infantry Regiment distinguished itself in the trenches of France.

14. _____ American losses in World War I were small compared to those of the other Allied nations.

Name _____ Date _____

Write Meanings to Words

Chapter 7 contains some words that may be new to you. Other words you have probably seen but are not sure of their meanings.

Listed here are sixteen words from the chapter. They are in the order in which they appear in the text. Go back and look at each word and the way it is used in a particular sentence. Then look up the words in a dictionary and write their meanings on the lines provided.

1. British Isles
   _____

2. blockade
   _____

3. liner
   _____

4. munitions
   _____

5. resumption
   _____

6. propaganda
   _____

7. embassy
   _____

8. unrestricted
   _____

9. proposed
   _____

10. draft
    _____

11. lottery
    _____

12. inducted
    _____

13. expeditionary
    _____

14. notorious
    _____

15. exploit
    _____

16. regiment
    _____

CHAPTER 8

Women Join the Fight

W orld War I was unique not only because it eventually involved a large part of the world. It was also different in that women assumed roles and took on tasks they had previously been denied.

In all the wars prior to World War I, the role of women had been severely limited. A few served as nurses on the battlefronts, but most stayed home and contributed as best they could. Some women knitted socks. Others made and rolled bandages. Still others fed and cared for wounded soldiers. A few, to be sure, disguised themselves as men and marched off to fight. But women, for the most part, were expected to stay home and perform their duties as wives and mothers.

World War I changed all that. With so many men off fighting the war, women were drawn into the workforce in record numbers. They worked as streetcar conductors and drove buses and ambulances. They became bank tellers, executives, and department managers. They worked in armaments factories making shells and ammunition. They planted fields and harvested crops. The kinds of jobs they successfully handled were amazing considering that before the war, women had mostly worked as domestic servants.

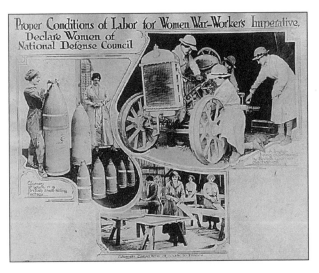

Women especially made their presence felt in the munitions industry. In France, more than a million women were working in defense-type jobs by 1918. In Austria-Hungary, more than 42 percent of all workers in heavy industry were women. This number was even higher in Germany. There, 55 percent of industrial workers were women. About 700,000 women labored in munitions factories for as many as 60 hours a week. More than 28,000 worked in the huge Krupps armaments plant alone.

British and French women undertaking heavy war work, ca. 1917.

Typical of women workers were the "munitionettes." This was the name applied to the women who worked in the munitions factories of England. They were also known as "canaries" because daily handling of shell powder turned their skin a bright yellow. By the end of the war, their number had grown to almost a million, and they were producing almost 80 percent of the shells and weapons used by the British army.

From *Everyday Life: World War I* © Good Year Books. This page may be reproduced for classroom use only by the actual purchaser of the book. www.goodyearbooks.com

Work in a munitions factory was highly dangerous. More than two hundred Englishwomen were killed when shells exploded. Others would suffer for years from poisoning caused by handling dangerous chemicals. Working conditions in munitions plants in countries such as Austria-Hungary was even worse. In addition to being dangerous, conditions were similar to those of the Industrial Revolution. Women often collapsed at their machines from exhaustion and hunger. Those who managed to stay on their feet found it impossible to work in winter, as factories were often unheated. Small wonder that these women sometimes fought and screamed at each other in sheer desperation.

Not all women worked in factories or at other jobs on the home front. Some went into battle as nurses. Two of the most famous were Elsie Knocker and Mairi Chisholm.

Elsie Knocker was a twenty-nine-year-old English divorcee. Mairi Chisholm was a brazen 18-year-old Scottish girl who drove her motorbike from Scotland to England to join up with an ambulance corps being sent to help the Belgian army. They worked with the ambulance corps for awhile and then decided to set up a front-line first aid station in the Belgian village of Pervyse. They had observed that many soldiers who were wounded in the trenches died from shock before they could be transported to a rear hospital. They believed they could save many lives if they set up an aid station close to the trenches.

Women taking the place of men working on the Great Northern Railway at Great Falls, Montana, ca. 1918.

Because she was a trained nurse, Elsie Knocker took care of most of the medical work. Mairi Chisholm mostly drove the ambulance. Sometimes the two actually carried wounded men across No Man's Land to their nearby aid station. Several times they made brief trips to England to raise new funds for their station. They became known as the "Women of Pervyse."

They stayed at their work in Pervyse until they were both gassed in March 1918. For their efforts to save the wounded, they were awarded Belgian's Military Medal and the Belgian Order of Leopold.

Women in the United States also made their way to the battlefronts. This was in spite of an order by General Pershing forbidding American women to come to France. He at first limited his order to female relatives of soldiers. Later, he extended the order to include all women except a few nurses and telephone operators. Like most men at the time, he saw a woman's only place as in the home.

Never was an order so ignored. By war's end, some twenty-five thousand women had sailed to France. They ranged in age from twenty-one to older than sixty. About half of them became nurses. The others drove ambulances or ran canteens for soldiers. A few even became war correspondents.

The determination of American women to take part in the war is perhaps best illustrated by Shirley Millard, a young New Yorker who wanted to get to France at any cost. Her chance came when she learned that the French were in dire need of nurses. The fact that she knew absolutely nothing about nursing mattered little to her. She could speak fluent French, and she figured she could read a nursing book during the eight-day voyage across the Atlantic.

When Shirley arrived in France, she managed to bluff French authorities into thinking she was, in fact, a nurse. Almost immediately she found herself in a truck bound for the front. She soon arrived at a chateau (house) that served as a field hospital, and for the first time she saw the reality of war. She gasped at wounded men without arms, legs, or eyes. But once again, her bravery and confidence served her well. At first, she was taken aback when a doctor shoved a hypodermic needle in her hand and told her to give every wounded soldier who arrived a tetanus shot. Now, Shirley had not only never given a shot, she had never *received* one. Any other person might have panicked at the thought. But not Shirley. She watched another nurse give several shots, and although on her first attempt she bent the needle, she quickly picked up the technique.

While Shirley Millard and others served their countries as nurses, some women actually fought. Along with several hundred other Russian women, Maria Bochkareva fought in the trenches alongside men. She later obtained permission from Czar Nicholas II to organize an all-female battalion. It was called the Battalion of Death. Its members shaved their heads and wore regular army uniforms.

It is easy to suppose that the women who joined the Battalion of Death were peasant women. After all, life on the farm offered nothing but hard work and drudgery. But the women who volunteered came from all walks of life. They included stenographers, dressmakers, and university students. Many were from the middle class. While some joined the battalion to help defend their country, others admitted that they enlisted to escape the humdrum routine of their daily lives.

Perhaps the most famous female soldier of World War I was Flora Sandes. She started off as a nurse working with the Serbian army and ended up a decorated soldier. How she came to be first a corporal and later an officer makes for an interesting story.

Flora Sandes was the daughter of an Irish clergyman who moved to England in the 1870s. She was a true tomboy, having announced as a little girl that she wished she had been born a boy. She learned to ride and shoot, and she swore she would never marry. She almost held true to this vow. She did not marry until she was fifty-one!

Flora had to decide on a means of earning a living, and she grudgingly took a job as a secretary. As a diversion, she drove an old French racing car. In her spare time, she took a nursing course. When World War I broke out, she was ready and eager to go.

On August 12, 1914, Flora and thirty-six other nurses left London by ship, bound for Serbia. She had joined an ambulance unit in the Serbian army. At the time, she was almost forty years old. She served with the ambulance unit for awhile, and then she was accepted into the Serbian army as a regular soldier. This was not unusual; a number of Serbian women fought with male troops on the front lines.

Flora was soon promoted to corporal. She became a favorite with her regiment when she convinced British and French authorities to supply them with new uniforms. The grateful men of her own company composed an address praising her efforts on their behalf. The address ended with: "Long life to our ally England!/Long Life to Serbia!/Long life to their heroic Armies!/Long life to noble Miss Sandes!"

In 1916, Flora Sandes was wounded by a grenade in a hand-to-hand battle with the enemy. Afterward, she returned to her original duties as an army nurse. She was promoted to sergeant-major and awarded Serbia's highest military decoration, the King George Star. In 1919, she was commissioned the first woman officer in the Serbian army. She remained in the army until she retired, eventually attaining the rank of major. In 1927, she married Sergeant Yurie Yudenich. Upon his death in 1941, she returned to England, where she died in 1956.

Sgt. Maj. Flora Sandes, who went to Serbia as a nurse and ended up fighting in the Serbian army.

This chapter mentions only a few of the brave women who served in World War I. There were many others.

Name _____ Date _____

Complete a Questionnaire

Here are statements about women in the military. Indicate whether you agree or disagree by circling the appropriate response at the beginning of each. On the lines provided, explain why you feel as you do.

1. (Agree/Disagree)   Women have no place in the military.

    _____

    _____

    _____

2. (Agree/Disagree)   The duties of women who join the armed forces should be limited to such tasks as desk work and nursing.

    _____

    _____

    _____

3. (Agree/Disagree)   Women should never be assigned to a combat area.

    _____

    _____

    _____

4. (Agree/Disagree)   Women should fight as soldiers on the front lines as men do.

    _____

    _____

    _____

5. (Agree/Disagree)   Women should be given command opportunities and promotions just as men are given.

    _____

    _____

    _____

Name _____ Date _____

Fill in a Venn Diagram

Fill in the Venn diagram below to compare the roles of women in World War I with those of women in previous wars. Write facts about each in the appropriate place. List characteristics common to both where the circles overlap.

World War I

Both

Previous Wars

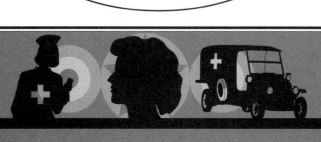

Name _____ Date _____

State Your Case in a Letter

Like women in Europe, American women filled jobs vacated by men who went off to fight in 1917. They performed the kinds of work that men had thought women could not do, and they performed well.

When the war ended in 1918 and the soldiers came home, women were expected to step aside and give their jobs back to men. After all, a woman's place was "in the home." Women resented this attitude, and they resented losing the freedom to work that the war had afforded them.

If you are a girl, pretend you are one of these women who has lost her job. Write a letter to a friend saying how unfair you think this is. Give reasons why you think you should be allowed to continue working.

If you are a boy, pretend you are one of the returning soldiers. Write a letter to a friend explaining why you are entitled to have your job back.

Date _____

Dear _____,

_____

_____

_____

_____

_____

_____

_____

_____

_____

_____

_____

_____

_____

_____

_____

_____

_____

_____

_____

_____

_____

Sincerely,

_____

Name _____   *Date* _____

Recall Information You Have Read

Without looking back over the chapter, write your best answers to these questions.

1. Why were so many job opportunities open to women during World War I?

   _____
   _____
   _____
   _____

2. Why were the women who worked in England's munitions plants called "canaries"?

   _____
   _____
   _____
   _____

3. Describe the activities of the Women of Pervyse.

   _____
   _____
   _____
   _____

4. What was the Battalion of Death?

   _____
   _____
   _____
   _____

5. How did Flora Sandes, an Englishwoman, come to be a soldier in the Serbian army? Briefly describe her career as such.

   _____
   _____
   _____
   _____

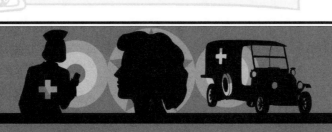

CHAPTER 9

The Home Fronts

Every war has two fronts. There is the front where the actual fighting takes place—the battlefront—and there is the home front. The latter refers to the contributions and sacrifices made by civilians to support the troops in combat. Without the assistance of the home front, soldiers would be hard-pressed to carry on a war.

The amazing thing about civilians on the home front is that they usually accept hardships and shortages without complaint. They also accept giving their government almost absolute powers to carry on the war. In times of crisis, a government will often assume control of major means of production and transportation. This has been true of the United States as well as other countries. Civilians realize that some kind of centralized authority is necessary if a war is to be brought to a satisfactory conclusion.

U.S. Food Administration photo of French women hitched to the plough. All agriculture in France rested on the shoulders of French women during the war.

In various ways, however, the home front in World War I was different from that of other wars. There were two reasons for this. The first was that no country on either side saw any reason to stockpile food and raw materials. After all, the war was not expected to last more than a few weeks or months. Remember how the Kaiser assured the German people that the troops would be "home before the leaves fall"?

Another factor that made the home front different was that each side blockaded the other. The Central Powers were determined to prevent food and other supplies from reaching English and French ports. The English and French were just as determined to keep much-needed supplies from reaching Germany and her allies. The strength of the British navy and the activity of German U-boats made the blockading of the respective coasts an effective weapon.

The blockades had little impact at first. But by the end of 1915, their effects were being felt by all of the nations. Russia and Austria-Hungary, the two least industrialized countries, were especially vulnerable. It did not help that Russian policy was in part determined by Rasputin, who, as you learned in chapter 3, greatly influenced Czar Nicholas and his wife. Any reforms (changes) that might have helped the Russian people never got off the ground.

From Everyday Life: World War I © Good Year Books. This page may be reproduced for classroom use only by the actual purchaser of the book. www.goodyearbooks.com

Even the industrialized countries felt the sting of the blockade. Germany was among the first to issue ration cards. Ration cards contained coupons that allowed people to purchase limited amounts of items in short supply. The items included such staples as sugar, tea, margarine, butter, meat, and cheese, as well as oil and coal for heating. Potatoes, cereal, and soap were also rationed in some places. When meat was hard to get, Germans were encouraged to go fishing and save meat for the troops at the front. Sometimes they had to settle for such "delicacies" as pickled walrus and boiled crow! Many Germans got by on turnips and beets.

As was true in other countries, Germans stood in long lines to receive rationed food and other goods. Women would arise in the middle of the night and line up for food. They sometimes took their knitting and sewing with them to pass the time.

Shortages in England became severe in 1917. In February of that year, German U-boats sank 230 ships carrying food and other supplies. Still, the British government did not introduce rationing until January 1918. They did so because of rumors circulating that the country was running out of food. This resulted in a panic that caused people to buy everything they could find. The introduction of rationing by the Ministry of Food ended such panic buying.

School children holding one of the large heads of cabbage raised in the War garden of New York City's Public School 88, ca. 1918. The garden yielded more than $500 worth of produce.

The United States' turn to conserve food and other supplies came in 1917. A poster put out by the U.S. Food Administration summed up what was expected of people. It challenged Americans to use four items sparingly: wheat, meat, sugar, and fats. Corn was suggested as a substitute for wheat. Meat could be replaced by fish and beans, and syrup could be substituted for sugar. As for fats, people were instructed to use just enough for their needs.

Americans quickly got used to rationing and restrictions. There were "Meatless Mondays" and "Wheatless Wednesdays." Driving an automobile was forbidden on Sundays and holidays, and there was no heat on certain days. This latter rule was especially difficult because of the severity of the winter of 1917–18. Not only was it extremely cold, but the United States, like nations elsewhere, was caught in the grips of a terrible flu pandemic. A pandemic is an epidemic that spreads worldwide.

Another issue facing the home fronts concerned conscientious objectors. You have learned from reading about Sergeant York that a conscientious objector is a person who rejects war on moral grounds. Such a person believes it is wrong to kill another person. Conscientious objectors have sometimes been jailed for their beliefs.

Conscientious objectors in England were subject to ridicule and scorn. They were singled out because England, until 1916, relied on an all-volunteer army, and it needed all the manpower it could muster. Men who refused to take up arms were considered slackers. Many did, however, agree to military service if they were assured they would not have to fight. Such men worked in hospitals, kitchens, and on farms.

In the United States, conscientious objectors were joined in their opposition to the war by pacifists and socialists. Pacifists believe that all wars are evil. Socialists maintain that war is nothing by a struggle between capitalist countries, and they want no part of it. Pacifists and socialists found themselves being persecuted. The same was true of people with German names. Many in these groups lost their jobs or saw their businesses ruined either by boycotts (when people refuse to buy a product or patronize a business) or vandalism. Some were beaten and even tarred and feathered.

Some Americans went even farther in their hatred of anything German. In some places, the German language and German music were forbidden. In others, towns with German names were changed. A town named Berlin might become "Liberty" while one named New Hamburg might be changed to "New Liberty." Even foods and animals were not exempt. Sauerkraut, a typical German dish made from cabbage, was renamed "liberty cabbage." And the dachshund, the low-slung, short-legged dog often associated with Germany, was called the "liberty pup."

About a third of the conscientious objectors in the United States eventually saw some kind of service. Only 540 of the original 64,693 men who had registered as conscientious objectors were imprisoned. Some 20,000 were drafted, and 16,000 were convinced they should fight. Most of the remainder were assigned to duty in the medical crops or in other non-fighting roles. Those who would not even accept these duties became agricultural laborers.

Another characteristic of life on the home fronts was the selling of war bonds to finance the war. No nation could raise enough money through taxation, so its citizens were encouraged to buy bonds. A bond is no more than a loan to a government or organization. People who buy bonds are lending

money in return for interest they will receive at a later date. In the United States, war bonds were called Liberty Bonds. Posters encouraged people to buy them to help the war effort. Rallies were held to stir up patriotism and to sell bonds as quickly as possible. Movie stars such as Douglas Fairbanks and Mary Pickford donated their time at these rallies. Buying bonds came to be seen as a patriotic duty.

As the war was winding down in the summer and fall of 1918, home fronts everywhere were faced with a crisis far worse than shortages of food and other supplies. That crisis was the influenza pandemic of 1918. The illness was called the Spanish flu, but it might have begun in American army camps either in the United States or France. By the time it ended in 1919, it had spread worldwide. Sources place the number of deaths it caused at anywhere between twenty and a hundred million.

The influenza came in several waves. The first wave was relatively mild and caused little concern. Two succeeding waves, however, were characterized by a virus so powerful that its victims sometimes died within hours. People tried to ward off infection by wearing gauze face masks, but these proved to be totally ineffective. Doctors and nurses who wore them died just like everybody else.

"You Buy A Liberty Bond. Lest I perish. Get Behind The Government. Liberty Loan of 1917." The sale of Liberty Bonds helped raise money for the war effort.

The influenza pandemic of 1918–19 killed more people in one year than the four years of the bubonic plague killed from 1347–51. By the time it finally ended, it had devastated Europe and America. Some twenty-one million people in Europe died of the illness. Estimates place the number of deaths in the United States as high as 675,000. More American troops died from the flu than in the trenches of France. Small wonder that children in 1918 skipped rope to the rhyme:

I had a little bird,
Its name was Enza;
I opened the window,
And in-flu-Enza.

Name _____ Date _____

Finish a Home Front Story

In chapter 9, you learned about food shortages and other hardships faced by citizens on the home fronts. People lined up in cities to receive daily handouts of bread and other foodstuffs. With this in mind, complete a story that has been started for you. Expand on the story and give it an ending.

Frau (Mrs.) Schmidt and Frau Krohn were among the last to arrive at the bread line. The line stretched down the street and around a corner. They were not worried, however, because bread lines in Berlin were always long, and there was usually enough bread for everyone.

This morning was to prove different. When they finally reached the point where the bread was being distributed, they learned there was no more to be handed out. "Try the line over on Lietzenburgerstrasse," they were told.

The two ladies hurried several blocks over to Lietzenburgerstrasse. To their utter shock and disbelief, there was nothing to be had at that point either. All that day's bread ration was gone.

What would they to do now? Both ladies had sick, hungry children at home. There was nothing left to feed them. How would they cope?

_____

_____

_____

_____

_____

_____

_____

_____

_____

_____

_____

_____

_____

_____

Name _____   Date _____

Solve Some Pandemic Word Problems

Here are four word problems dealing with the terrible influenza pandemic of 1918–19. Space is provided for you to work each problem. Write your answers on the appropriate lines.

1. In 1918–19, the population of the United States was about 100,000,000. If a fourth of this number contracted influenza, how many people came down with the disease?

    _____ Answer

2. Some 675,000 Americans died during the influenza pandemic. Referring to your answer to the first question, what percent of those infected did not recover?

    _____ Answer

3. The world's population at the time of the pandemic was about 1.8 billion. If 70 million people worldwide died of the disease, what percent of the world's population does this number represent?

    _____ Answer

4. About 23 percent of deaths worldwide from influenza occurred in India. How many died in that country?

    _____ Answer

Name _____ Date _____

Create a Dialogue

In chapter 9 you learned that a pacifist is someone who is against war for any reason. In the eyes of a pacifist, all wars are evil.

On the lines opposite, create a dialogue (conversation) that might have taken place between a pacifist and a person who supported the United States going to war in 1917. Have each person give reasons to support the way he or she feels.

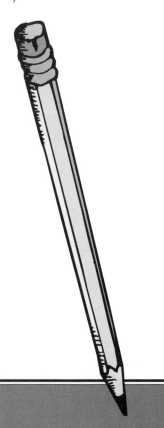

From *Everyday Life: World War I* © Good Year Books. This page may be reproduced for classroom use only by the actual purchaser of the book. www.goodyearbooks.com

Name _____ Date _____

Make False Statements True

All the statements on this page are false. Change the words in *italics* to make them true. Write the replacement words on the lines following the statements.

1. Rasputin, who called himself a monk, came to have much influence on the government of *Austria-Hungary*.

   _____

2. A *fascist* sees war as a conflict between capitalistic nations.

   _____

3. Pacifists believe that all wars are *good*.

   _____

4. "Liberty cabbage" is what Americans came to call *relish*.

   _____

5. To help finance the war, governments encouraged their citizens to buy *ration cards*.

   _____

6. Americans referred to the *German shepherd* as the "liberty pup."

   _____

7. A *strike* is an action in which people refuse to buy a product or support a business.

   _____

8. During World War I, Americans were encouraged to use *beans* as a substitute for wheat.

   _____

9. The deadly virus that emerged in 1918 was referred to as the *French* flu.

   _____

10. An epidemic is called a pandemic when it spreads *nationwide*.

    _____

11. A blockade is a military tactic carried out by soldiers *on the ground*.

    _____

BEANS

WHEAT

CHAPTER 10

Unusual and Interesting Stories

The history of World War I contains a treasure house of unusual stories and events. Some are tragic. Others are amusing. A few are heartwarming. All are interesting.

Many of the anecdotes (stories) connected with World War I center around the First Battle of the Marne in 1914. One story has to do with the uniform worn by French infantrymen. By the time the fighting bogged down into trench warfare, all the other nations involved had abandoned colorful-type dress for something more befitting for slugging it out in muddy ditches. In other words, they changed to either khaki or gray—colors closely resembling the mud they had to deal with.

But not the French. Tradition held that the French soldier march off to war in the kind of uniform worn in previous wars. The most outrageous part of this uniform was its baggy red trousers. If anything would make a trooper stand out among the dirt and mud of the battlefield, it was being saddled with bright red pants! While the French soldiers no doubt hated this attire, the Germans on the western front must have loved it. Red pants provided an easy target for riflemen and machine gunners.

Whether it was winter or summer, French soldiers wore a long, heavy greatcoat and long underwear. But the most uncomfortable part of their dress might have been their boots. Historians maintain that no soldier in any other army would have consented to wear such uncomfortable boots. French soldiers called them *brodequins,* and with good reason. The brodequin was the name of an ancient instrument of torture.

To top it off, the French soldier carried a kit or pack that weighed up to 66 pounds. Then, on top of this kit, he had to carry kindling wood at all times. The kindling wood was for making fires when the troops stopped to camp. (This was in the early days of the war, before trench warfare.) It is easy to see how delighted French soldiers were when their government finally introduced uniforms that replaced the baggy red trousers and the heavy pack.

Another story from the war involved a German officer. Again, before the beginning of trench warfare, troops moved back and forth. Sometimes neither side was quite sure who controlled a certain town. This particular German officer rode into the wrong town at the wrong time.

One day, the officer and his driver stopped at the post office in the French town of La Fere. The officer assumed that the town was in German hands. His

driver observed a number of unarmed French soldiers standing around, but he took them to be prisoners. The German officer went into the post office and mailed a number of postcards. The cards read: "Marvelous success! The French and British are running away like rabbits!" Apparently satisfied with passing along such news, he left the post office and quickly became a prisoner of war. The town was under French control.

One story associated with World War I concerned the first Christmas spent on the western front. Soldiers from both sides climbed out of the trenches and walked into No Man's Land. There they exchanged gifts of chocolate, tobacco, and cigarettes and sang Christmas carols. The Germans had even set up lighted Christmas trees along their trenches. Several soccer games between German and British troops were even staged. Such fraternization was similar to that of Union and Confederate soldiers during the American Civil War. After that first Christmas, however, angry Allied commanders issued orders to shoot anyone trying to fraternize with the Germans.

World War I's unsung heroes were dogs, and there are amazing tales of their accomplishments. The Germans used about thirty thousand trained dogs, while the French had some twenty thousand. When the United States entered the war, it borrowed dogs that had been trained by the French and British.

A dog wearing a message tube. Messages carried by dogs helped military units stay in touch.

Dogs served many purposes. Most were used as messengers and sentries, but many performed a variety of other tasks. Some carried ammunition and food to soldiers in the trenches. Others were trained as ratters, their job being to reduce the number of rats in the trenches. Then there were small Cigarette Dogs, who braved enemy fire to carry tobacco to the troops. There were few tasks dogs could not perform if properly trained.

Of special importance were the Red Cross Casualty Dogs. Sometimes they were called Mercy Dogs. They were outfitted with saddlebags containing medical supplies. They located many a wounded soldier, and there is no doubt that the contents of their bags saved lives. Some dogs were even trained to bring back a wounded man's helmet or piece of clothing to alert others of his whereabouts.

A number of individual dog heroes stand out. One was a French Red Cross dog named Prusco. Prusco was credited with saving the lives of more

than a hundred men in a single day. He dragged some of these wounded men back to the safety of the trenches.

Another memorable dog was Cabot. Cabot distinguished himself one night by intercepting a German messenger dog and ripping away and stealing the metal tube attached to its collar! The tube contained important German military messages that proved vital to the French.

Some sources maintain that the most famous dog of the war was Satan. Satan was a big, black dog credited with saving a French garrison from destruction at the battle of Verdun. With the town surrounded and continually pounded by German shells, the situation looked hopeless indeed. When the last of the carrier pigeons was killed, there was no way to send a message to the rear instructing gunners to silence a certain German battery.

One night French soldiers spotted a black speck in the distance running like mad toward the town. After some time, they identified the speck as the messenger dog named Satan. But before Satan could zigzag his way through murderous German fire, he was hit in one of his back legs. Did Satan give up? Absolutely not! He dragged his wounded body the rest of the way into town with his valuable cargo: two baskets on his back, each containing a very frightened pigeon. The addition of the pigeons enabled the French in the town to send messages to rear gunners to knock out the German guns that had been battering the place to pieces. Thus it was that a messenger dog saved Verdun from falling.

Few stories of World War I are more intriguing than the circumstances surrounding the death of Rasputin, the monk living at Nicholas II's court. Many Russians despised Rasputin, whose real name was Grigori Yefimovich. (*Rasputin* was a nickname meaning "dissolute," which refers to a person who leads an immoral life.) They resented his meddling in governmental affairs. The aristocracy, or noble class, especially despised him. He seldom bathed, he was drunk much of the time, and he was a notorious woman chaser. More than anyone, he was blamed for Russia's poor showing in World War I and for the lack of reforms to help the poor. It is not surprising that in late 1916 a small group of aristocrats conspired to kill him.

Attaching a message to a Signal Corps carrier pigeon, ca. 1917.

The conspiracy was led by Prince Felix Yussupov. As a relative of the czar, Yussupov had easy access to Rasputin and was therefore in a position to kill him. On December 16, 1916, the prince and four others invited the monk to a late-night supper at the prince's palace. They served him cakes injected with cyanide of potassium and glass after glass of wine containing the same poison. Rasputin had his fill of both, and nothing happened. He had eaten enough poisoned cake and drunk enough poisoned wine to kill several men. But nothing happened!

Yussupov and the others stared in disbelief. Then Yussupov panicked and left the room. He returned with a revolver and shot Rasputin at point blank range. At this, the monk, instead of dying, began to crawl toward Yussupov screaming at the top of his lungs. The terrified killers then shot him again and began to beat and stab him. Thinking him finally dead, they bound the body with rope and rolled it up in a carpet. They then proceeded to the Neva River and dumped the body in the water.

The strange story of the murder of Rasputin did not end there. When his body was later retrieved from the river and examined, it was discovered that his lungs were filled with water. Poison, shooting, beating, and stabbing had not killed the monk! He had drowned!

These are but a few of the unusual stories associated with World War I. There are, of course, many more, as you can see in these photographs.

The "Human Squirrel" did many daring "stunts" for the benefit of War Relief Funds in New York City. He is shown above Times Square, ca. 1918.

Marjorie Stinson, the only woman to be granted a pilot's license during the war by the Army & Navy Committee of Aeronautics, ca. 1917.

Hazel Carter of Douglas, Arizona, donned an Army uniform and stowed away on a ship to France to stay with her soldier husband. She was discovered and sent home. She died while her husband, Corporal John Carter, was still overseas, ca. 1918.

Name _____ Date _____

Complete a Vocabulary Exercise

Select the meaning of each word as it is used in chapter 10. Circle the letter of the correct meaning. The paragraph in which each word appears in the narrative is written in parentheses.

1. **abandoned** (paragraph 2)
   a. deserted
   b. given up entirely
   c. wicked

2. **front** (paragraph 3)
   a. the first part
   b. site where battles take place
   c. manner of looking

3. **instrument** (paragraph 4)
   a. means
   b. device for producing musical sounds
   c. tool

4. **introduced** (paragraph 5)
   a. made two people acquainted with each other
   b. brought in or started
   c. brought forward for consideration

5. **battery** (paragraph 14)
   a. a unit of artillery
   b. an electric cell
   c. the unlawful beating of another person

6. **carrier** (paragraph 14)
   a. postman
   b. person who transmits disease
   c. thing that carries something

7. **fire** (paragraph 15)
   a. heat of feeling
   b. the shooting or discharge of guns
   c. something burning

8. **bound** (paragraph 19)
   a. under some obligation
   b. certain
   c. tied fast

Name _____ Date _____

Make a Shoe Box Diorama

Life in the trenches of World War I was not all fighting. Soldiers, in fact, spent much of their time either in boredom or in taking care of necessary chores. There was even one time (as you learned in this chapter) in 1914 when German and Allied soldiers met in No Man's Land and celebrated Christmas together.

With this Christmas incident in mind, make a shoe box diorama depicting the scene. Use your imagination in creating the appearance of the trenches and No Man's Land.

Materials That Will Be Helpful Include:

1. A large shoe box

2. Modeling clay

3. Small figurines of soldiers

4. Construction paper

5. Cardboard

6. Wire or something similar to fashion coiled barbed wire

7. Watercolors, crayons, or markers

8. Small tree saplings to serve as Christmas trees

9. Scissors

10. Glue or paste

Name _____ Date _____

Draw Conclusions from What You Read

Read each of the situations. Then, on the lines provided, write your own conclusions based on the questions asked.

1. You read in this chapter how German and Allied troops came out of the trenches at Christmas 1914, and celebrated the holiday together. They sang songs and exchanged gifts. They trimmed Christmas trees. They even played soccer. What does such fraternization tell you about these men? Do you think they might have felt differently once the shooting started again? Why or why not?

   _____

   _____

   _____

   _____

   _____

   _____

2. Soldiers often kept pets in the trenches with them. Even such an infamous person as Adolf Hitler, who served as a corporal in the German army in World War I, had a pet dog. What conclusion can you draw as to why soldiers would keep pets in such a dangerous environment? And as for Hitler, how could a person so attached to an animal (he was irate when it was later stolen) be so callous in being responsible for the deaths of millions of innocent people another world war later?

   _____

   _____

   _____

   _____

3. When news of Rasputin's death on December 16, 1916, reached the Duma—the Russian legislative body—delegates stood up and cheered. Why would sensible representatives hail what was in many ways a cold-blooded act of murder?

   _____

   _____

   _____

   _____

Name _____ Date _____

Create a Dialogue between French Soldiers

You have learned that the uniform worn by French soldiers at the beginning of World War I left much to be desired. Saddled with baggy red trousers, a heavy backpack, and a load of kindling wood, they must have provided comic relief to the enemy. In addition, whereas soldiers of most of the other nations involved were equipped with some kind of helmet, the French soldier had to make do with a *kepi*, a regular cap that offered no protection to the head. Surely French soldiers must have complained among themselves as they trudged into battle.

Create a dialogue that might have taken place between several soldiers as they plodded along in their outdated uniforms.

CHAPTER II

The Aftermath

At precisely 11 o'clock on the morning of November 11, 1918, the guns on all fronts fell silent. An armistice (cease-fire) was agreed upon to begin on the eleventh hour of the eleventh day of the eleventh month of that year. After four terrible years of bloodshed, World War I was over.

Soldiers on both sides came out of the trenches and celebrated. Souvenirs and personal items were exchanged. The Germans were happy to have cigarettes, soap, and food rations. Americans, for their part, came away with German medals, belt buckles, bayonets, and pistols. Riotous celebration came later. For now, giddy Americans were content to play such games of their childhood as hopscotch and blind man's bluff. With soldiers being killed almost up to the last minute, it is not hard to imagine their delirious excitement.

The announcement of the armistice on November 11, 1918, in Philadelphia, Pennsylvania. Thousands massed at the replica of the Statue of Liberty on Broad Street.

Crowds in cities throughout Europe rushed into the streets. Church bells rang. Bands played. People danced, sang, and waved flags. A few jumped up on benches and led renditions of popular Allied war songs. At an American officer training school in one French town, candidates got carried away and bombed each other's barracks with live grenades! No one was killed, but there were a number of injuries.

On the east coast of the United States, it was only 6 A.M. when the armistice began. News of the historic event took several hours to reach places like New York and Washington, D.C. When it did, Americans celebrated just as wildly as their European counterparts. President Wilson issued a statement, which included in part: "Everything for which America fought has been accomplished." It was a most memorable day.

After the celebrations ended, the world took stock of the damage and destruction caused by the fighting. What at the time was called the Great War was the deadliest and costliest in world history. Estimates place the number of people killed at twenty million. Of this number, from nine to ten million were

soldiers or other military personnel. Perhaps twice this number were wounded. Men came home maimed or disabled for life. Many had lost one or more limbs. Some had even lost most of their face. Never had a war caused such horror and suffering.

In spite of the death and destruction, the world, particularly Europe, where most of the fighting had taken place, could not immediately return to normal. Many problems had to be dealt with, such as the deadly flu pandemic of 1918–19. Another was the rise of bolshevism, or communism. In 1917 Russia had been taken over by Bolsheviks, and Germany was seriously threatened with a similar takeover after the war stopped. Then there was the break-up of empires ruled by the Germans, Austro-Hungarians, Ottoman Turks, and Russians. When these empires collapsed, a number of new nations appeared on the map of Europe. Whereas nations should have been eager to cooperate in the interest of peace, the realignment of boundaries caused tensions that helped lead to another war twenty years later.

Not the least of the problems facing European nations were hunger and starvation. Many factories and farms had been totally destroyed, and there was widespread unemployment. Starvation was magnified because the Allies continued their naval blockade even after the fighting stopped. Food and other supplies could not reach people who desperately needed them. In Vienna, which had been the capital of the Austro-Hungarian Empire, the situation was particularly bad. A doctor in the city reported that people were dying everywhere, many of them young children.

As in other countries, Vienna also faced the problem of not having enough wood with which to build coffins. With winter having set in, almost all wood went for heat. As a result, there were few coffins available to bury the dead. Children were buried in boxes, while grown-ups were interred in mass graves. They were stacked in rows with a layer or dirt and lime between the bodies.

Two months after World War I ended in November 1918, representatives of all of the Allied nations met at the palace of Versailles outside of Paris to hammer out the terms of peace. Russia was not invited, having dropped out of the war in 1917. None of the Central Power nations were invited either. The peace conference was led and dominated by four leaders who came to be called the Big Four. They were President Woodrow Wilson of the United States, Prime Minister David Lloyd George of Great Britain, Premier Georges Clemenceau of France, and Premier Vittorio Orlando of Italy.

Clemenceau of France was determined to make Germany pay for starting the war. Although the initial confrontation was between Austria-Hungary and Serbia, Germany's support of the Austro-Hungarians, in the eyes of Clemenceau, made war possible. He blamed the Germans for the terrible destruction of France's towns, cities, and countryside. He also blamed them for the death of almost one-half of all young French men in their twenties. He wanted to punish the Germans and prevent them from causing another war.

Everything Clemenceau stood for was contrary to the ideas of President Wilson. Wilson had drawn up what he called the Fourteen Points. This was an ambitious plan he hoped would preserve the peace and prevent future wars. But Clemenceau and other Allied nations wanted no part of a program that treated nations fairly and that did not humiliate the Germans.

The Council of Four of the Peace Conference: David Lloyd George of Britain, Vittorio Orlando of Italy, Georges Clemenceau of France, and Woodrow Wilson of the United States. They are shown here in Paris, France, on May 27, 1919.

The delegates assembled at Paris in 1919 forced Germany to sign the Treaty of Versailles. The terms of the treaty were harsh. Perhaps the Germans could have lived with being denied an air force and having limits placed on the size of their army and navy. They could also have accepted losing territory and overseas colonies. But what infuriated the Germans was their having to accept total responsibility for starting the war. They felt that other nations were just as responsible as they were. Being shamed and forced to pay reparations (war damages) of $33 billion to the Allied powers proved useful to Adolf Hitler in his rise to power a mere fourteen years later. Hitler was also helped by the fact that Germany had surrendered while still occupying large parts of France and Belgium; Germans didn't think Germany had really been "beaten" in the war, because it still held territory at war's end. Germans who shared Hitler's view felt that Germany had been "stabbed in the back" by the politicians then in control.

A major part of President Wilson's Fourteen Points program was the League of Nations. Wilson saw this forerunner of the United Nations as a way to maintain world peace. It might have succeeded except for two reasons. First, the league did not provide for an international police force to bring warring

nations into line. It could only apply pressure in other ways. One way was to encourage member nations to break off diplomatic relations with any nation that started a war. Another was to call for a blockade to keep vital supplies from getting into the ports of such a nation. Perhaps the league's strongest power was to impose economic sanctions. This meant that member nations would not buy or sell anything to a nation guilty of disrupting the peace. None of these measures, however, proved effective against Germany, Italy, and Japan as they geared up for World War II.

A second reason for the failure of the League of Nations to preserve the peace was that the United States never joined the organization. After World War I concluded, a spirit of isolationism spread throughout the United States. Many Americans wanted nothing more to do with the affairs of Europe or those of anywhere else in the world. They feared that joining the League would in time result in the United States having to go to war again. Based on this feeling, the U.S. Senate refused to ratify the Treaty of Versailles with Germany. And because the League of Nations was included as part of that treaty, the entry of the United States into the League was denied.

With the Senate voting against the League, President Wilson took to the road to try to convince the American people that the United States should join. Because this was before the age of air travel, he went by train. He left Washington, D.C., on September 3, 1919, and began a whirlwind tour through the Midwest and West. At each stop along the way, he spoke to the gathering crowd. Then the train sped on to the next stop. The pace was exhausting. After making a speech at Pueblo, Colorado, on September 25, the president collapsed from exhaustion. The remainder of the tour was canceled, and he was rushed back to the White House in Washington.

One week after collapsing in Colorado, President Wilson suffered a massive stroke. His wife, Edith, found him on the bathroom floor of their living quarters in the White House. The stroke left him partially paralyzed on his left side. He completed the remaining seventeen months of his presidency as an invalid. The seriousness of his condition was kept secret from the American public.

The refusal of the United States to join the League of Nations had a tremendous impact on world stability. With the nation's strongest power not a member, there was little to stop aggressor nations from having their way. Could the United States' presence in the League have prevented World War II? What do you think?

Name _____ Date _____

Write a Summary

On the lines provided, write a summary describing how everyday life in Europe (and later the United States) was affected by the advent of World War I. List all the ways you remember that were mentioned in the previous chapters.

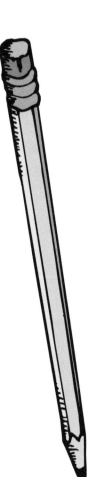

_____
_____
_____
_____
_____
_____
_____
_____
_____
_____
_____
_____
_____
_____
_____
_____
_____
_____
_____
_____
_____
_____
_____
_____
_____
_____
_____
_____
_____
_____

Name _____ Date _____

Solve an Aftermath Puzzle

ACROSS

1 A cease-fire or stop in fighting

6 Orlando was the premier of this country

7 Clemenceau was the premier of this country

9 Payments for war damages

11 Disease that killed millions in 1918–19

12 U.S. president during World War I

13 Country blamed for starting World War I

DOWN

2 _____ of Versailles

3 The League of _____

4 Number of years World War I lasted

5 Capital of Austria-Hungary

8 He came to power in Germany fourteen years after World War I

9 Country taken over by the Bolsheviks in 1917

10 The Fourteen _____

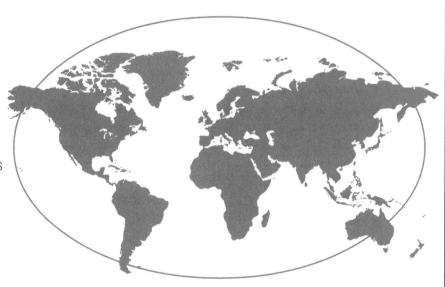

Name _____ Date _____

Write a Letter

Senator Henry Cabot Lodge of Massachusetts led the fight in the U.S. Senate in 1919 against the United States joining the League of Nations. Because of his efforts, the Senate did not ratify the Treaty of Versailles, and the establishment of the League of Nations was a major part of the treaty.

Pretend that you lived in Massachusetts in 1919 and that you supported President Wilson in insisting that the United States become a member of the league. With this in mind, write a letter to Senator Lodge giving reasons why you disagree with him and why you believe the United States should join.

Date _____

The Honorable Henry Cabot Lodge
United States Senate
Washington, D.C.

Dear Senator Lodge,

_____
_____
_____
_____
_____
_____
_____
_____
_____
_____
_____
_____
_____
_____
_____
_____
_____
_____

Sincerely,

_____
(your name)

From *Everyday Life: World War I* © Good Year Books. This page may be reproduced for classroom use only by the actual purchaser of the book. www.goodyearbooks.com

Name _____ Date _____

Interpret a Bar Graph

The bar graph shows in millions the number of casualties (those killed, wounded, or missing in action) suffered by six countries in World War I.

Review *mean*, *mode*, and *range* in your math text and, using the information from the graph, answer the questions at the bottom of the page.

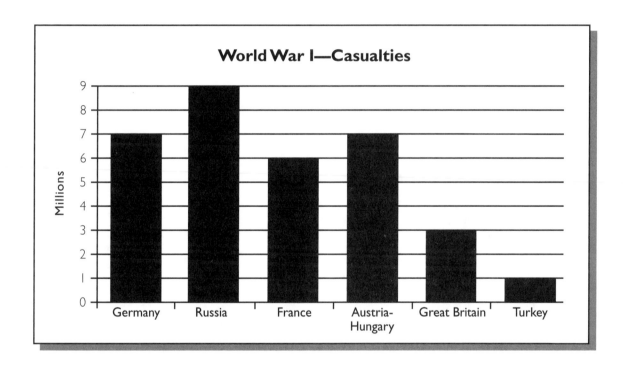

World War I—Casualties

1. What is the mean of the numbers provided? _____.

2. What is the mode? _____. Which countries do these numbers represent?
   _____

3. What is the range? _____

4. How many times greater was Russia's losses than those of Great Britain? _____

Answers to Activities

Chapter 1

Distinguish between Fact and Opinion
1. O 2. F 3. F 4. O 5. F 6. F 7. O 8. F
9. O 10. O 11. F

Draw a Map of the Balkan Peninsula
Balkan countries and their capitals are:
Croatia—Zagreb; Bosnia-Herzegovina—Sarajevo;
Serbia & Montenegro—Belgrade; Macedonia—
Skopje; Slovenia—Ljubljana; Albania—Tirana;
Bulgaria—Sofia; Greece—Athens

Interpret a Bar Graph
1. 3.3 2. Yes; 1 million 3. 5 million
4. Twice as great 5. Great Britain and Italy

Chapter 2

Make False Statements True
1. Otto von Bismarck 2. Austria-Hungary 3. Serbia
4. Bosnia 5. Sir Edward Grey 6. Triple Entente
7. Germany 8. Kaiser Wilhelm II of Germany
9. months 10. was sentenced to life in prison
11. Black Hand

Distinguish between Complete Sentences and Fragments
1. F 2. S 3. S 4. F 5. F 6. F 7. S 8. F

Chapter 3

Name Those Synonyms
Answers will vary. The following are possible responses.
1. chief; important 2. strict; harsh 3. rule; dominion
4. mistook; erred 5. dealing; delivering 6. controlled;
ruled 7. interfered; pried 8. hide; cover 9. outdo;
surpass 10. irritating; irksome 11. scare; frighten
12. depress; dishearten 13. promised; pledged
14. ruler; king 15. misfortune; misery 16. rebelled;
rose up 17. improvement; change 18. complaint;
accusation 19. expect; await 20. usual; common

Compare Monarchs
1. FJ 2. W 3. FJ 4. N 5. W 6. N 7. W 8. FJ 9. N
10. W 11. FJ 12. N 13. N 14. FJ 15. W 16. N

Convert Miles and Kilometers
1. 522 2. 986 3. 2107 4. 213 5. 2173

Chapter 4

Solve a New Weapons Puzzle
1. Germans 2. Bertha 3. water 4. Willie
5. Rickenbacker 6. Hiram 7. poison 8. chlorine
9. France 10. guns

Use Context Clues to Complete Sentences
different; soldiers; combat; charges; galloping;
bogged; cause; fire; user; staggering; minutes;
weapon; escaping; mustard; horrible; deadliest

Chapter 5

Compare and Contrast Wars
Answers will vary but should be similar to the following:
1. World War I made old methods of fighting, such as cavalry charges and infantry advancing in neat rows, obsolete. Trench warfare made great gains by either side impossible. This was mainly due to the advent of the machine gun.
2. Today wars are fought largely with aircraft and a reduced number of troops. Present-day armies have such modern weapons as "smart bombs" and "bunker busters."
3. Many people thought that the death and destruction caused by World War I was so terrible that the world would never go to war again.

Recall Information You Have Read
1. The Schlieffen Plan was an attempt to take Paris by invading neutral Belgium and encircling the French army.
2. The Battle of the Marne
3. No Man's Land was the area between the opposing trenches.
4. To "go over the top" meant to leave the trench and start advancing across No Man's Land.
5. They were on higher, drier land. They were also better constructed.
6. Trench fever was caused by lice.
7. Trench foot was a fungal infection. It was caused by soldiers having to stand for long periods of time in water. It often led to gangrene and amputation.

From *Everyday Life: World War I* © Good Year Books. This page may be reproduced for classroom use only by the actual purchaser of the book. www.goodyearbooks.com

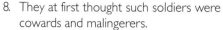

8. They at first thought such soldiers were cowards and malingerers.
9. Rats were attracted to the trenches by the smell of food and dead bodies.
10. Trenches were dug in zigzag fashion to prevent the enemy from lobbing in shells and killing a large number of troops at one time.

Chapter 6

Solve a Battle Puzzle

Across: 5. Tannenberg 6. Germany 7. Foch 8. Denmark 11. Paris 12. Jutland 13. Cambrai 14. Somme

Down: 1. Tennessee 2. Marne 3. Verdun 4. France 9. Russians 10. Belgium

Solve Four Word Problems

1. 35% 2. 3,000 3. 20 weeks 4. 56%

Chapter 7

Interpret Patriotic Verses

Answers should resemble the folowing:
1. She is proud for her son to serve his country.
2. They urge a young man to enlist.
3. These lines say that the United States is confident that its entry into the war will turn the tide.

Distinguish between Fact and Opinion

1. O 2. F 3. O 4. O 5. F 6. F 7. O 8. O 9. F 10. O 11. O 12. F 13. F 14. F

Write Meanings to Words

Definitions should resemble the following:
1. Great Britain, Ireland, and nearby islands
2. blocking a place with ships to prevent supplies from entering or leaving
3. a ship belonging to a transportation system
4. materiel used in war (guns, bombs, etc.)
5. starting up again
6. a systematic effort to spread opinions or beliefs
7. the official residence or office of an ambassador to a foreign country
8. placing no restrictions or limits on
9. suggested; put forward for consideration
10. selection of persons for some special purpose (soldiers, for example)
11. drawing of lots (names) for selecting persons to serve

12. enrolled in military service
13. making up an expedition, a journey for some special purpose
14. having a bad reputation
15. a bold act; a daring deed
16. military unit consisting of several battalions or squadrons

Chapter 8

Fill in a Venn Diagram

Answers will vary but should resemble the following:
World War I: worked in factories; drove ambulances; some fought as soldiers
Both: served as nurses; helped on the home front
Previous Wars: most stayed home; made bandages; knitted socks, etc.

Recall Information You Have Read

Answers should resemble the following:
1. Men were called into the military to fight in the war.
2. Their skin turned yellow from handling shell powder.
3. They set up an aid station in Belgium just behind the front lines. They personally brought or carried wounded soldiers from No Man's Land to the station, saving some from dying from shock.
4. The Battalion of Death was an army group of Russian women organized to fight alongside the men on the front lines.
5. Flora Sandes first went to Serbia as a member of an ambulance unit. Then she was accepted into the Serbian army as a soldier. She fought well, and she was promoted a number of times. She retired as a major.

Chapter 9

Solve Some Pandemic Word Problems

1. 2,500,000 2. .027 percent 3. .039 percent 4. about 16,000,000

Make False Statements True

1. Russia 2. socialist 3. evil or bad 4. sauerkraut 5. bonds 6. Dachshund 7. boycott 8. corn 9. Spanish 10. worldwide 11. in ships (or submarines)

Chapter 10

Complete a Vocabulary Exercise

1. b 2. b 3. a 4. b 5. a 6. c 7. b 8. c

Chapter 11

Solve an Aftermath Puzzle

Across: 1. armistice 6. Italy 7. France
9. reparations 11. flu 12. Wilson 13. Germany
Down: 2. Treaty 3. Nations 4. four 5. Vienna
8. Hitler 9. Russia 10. Points

Interpret a Bar Graph

1. 5.5 million 2. 7 million; Germany and Austria-
Hungary 3. 8 million 4. 3 times

Additional Resources

Books

Axelrod, Alan. *The Complete Idiot's Guide to World War I*. Indianapolis: Alpha Books, 2000.

Becker, Annette, and Stephane Audoin-Rouzeau. *14–18: Understanding the Great War*. New York: Hill and Wang, 2002.

Fleming, Thomas. *The Illusion of Victory: America in World War I*. New York: Basic Books, 2003.

Howard, Michael. *The First World War*. New York: Oxford University Press, 2002.

Massie, Robert K. *Nicholas and Alexandra*. New York: Atheneum, 1967.

Mitchell, David. *Monstrous Regiment: The Story of the Women of the First World War*. New York: Macmillan, 1965.

Strachan, Hew, ed. *The Oxford Illustrated History of the First World War*. Oxford: Oxford University Press, 1998.

Tuchman, Barbara W. *The Guns of August*. New York: Macmillan, 1962.

Wilmott, H. P. *World War I*. New York: Dorling Kindersley Publishing, 2003.

Web Sites

British Broadcasting Company. "World War One." http://www.bbc.co.uk/history/war/wwone/index.shtml

Caddick-Adams, Peter. "Women at War." http://www.bbc.co.uk/history/lj/wars/j/women_08.shtml

Community Television of Southern California. "1914–1918: The Great War and the Shaping of the 20th Century." http://www.pbs.org/greatwar

Encyclopedia of the First World War. "Women and War." http://www.spartacus.schoolnet.co.uk/FWWwomen.htm

Great War Society. "World War I, Trenches on the Web." http://www.worldwar1.com/

Hahn 50th Air Police Squadron, K-9 Section. "The Great War—1914–1915." http://community-2.webtv.net/Hahn-50thAp-K9/K9History2/

History Channel. "Encyclopedia: World War I." http://www.historychannel.com/thcsearch/thc_resourcedetail.do?encyc_id=226139

Wilson, Capt. Barbara A., USAF. "Women in World War One." http://userpages.aug.com/captbarb/femvets4.html